Healing Voices

Healing Voices

A Narrative of the Acts of God in The Christian and Missionary Alliance

Christian Publications, Inc.
Camp Hill, Pennsylvania

Christian Publications, Inc.
3825 Hartzdale Drive, Camp Hill, PA 17011
www.cpi-horizon.com
www.christianpublications.com

ISBN: 0-87509-790-1

00 01 02 03 04 5 4 3 2 1

Printed in the United States of America

Dedication

This book is dedicated to Dr. Keith M. Bailey, whose book, ***Divine Healing: The Children's Bread,*** *has schooled a generation of Alliance ordinands and has taken all his readers closer to the hem of Jesus' garment.*

The *Voices* Series

Prayer Voices
Holiness Voices
Missionary Voices
Voices on the Glory
Church-Planting Voices
Healing Voices
Voices from a Changing America

Contents

Divine Healing: The Power, the Pain and the Promise

Divine Healing: Looking to the Future

Foreword

H*ealing Voices* has been a long time coming. From the very first of the *Voices* series, we knew we would be doing *Healing Voices*. The material from which to choose has been immense. For those whose material does not appear here, and you are very many, thanks for making your story available, too.

This book ranges from A.B. Simpson's solid-rock principles all the way to the pain of those who were not healed. Mitch Schultz's poignant story needs to be as much a part of any book on divine healing as do the marvelous deliverances from even cancer recorded here. Clarence Shrier was a favorite of mine; his meetings were frequently marked by the presence of the Lord in healing power. Steve Adams, editor of *Alliance Life*, has helped from a distance and his contribution is much appreciated. Judy Harris, my assistant, has labored lovingly over these pages while her own dad has been undergoing treatment. Typesetting and prayer do go together.

Wherever this book goes, there will be healings and deliverances. We know that. All glory to the Lamb of God in advance for what He will do with His Word and with these honest testimonials.

K. Neill Foster
Publisher
April 2000

Divine Healing:
A Narrative of the Acts of God in
The Christian and Missionary Alliance

CHAPTER

1

Principles of Divine Healing

By A.B. Simpson

There are certain principles underlying the teachings of the Holy Scriptures with respect to healing that are important to understand. When rightly comprehended, they are most helpful to intelligent faith.

The causes of disease and suffering are distinctly traced to the Fall and the sinful state of man. If sickness were part of the natural constitution of things, then we might meet it wholly on natural grounds and by natural means. But if it be part of the curse of sin, it must have its true remedy in the great Redemption. That sickness is the result of the Fall and one of the fruits of sin, no one can surely question. Death, we are told, has passed upon all, for all have sinned, and the greater includes the less.

Sickness is named among the curses that God was to send for Israel's sin (Deuteronomy 28:58–61). Again, sickness is distinctly connected with Satan's personal agency. He was the direct instrument of Job's suffering; and our Lord definitely attributed the diseases of His time directly to satanic power. It was Satan who bound the paralyzed woman "these eighteen years." It was demonic influence that held and crushed the bodies and souls of those Christ delivered. If sickness is the result of a spirit agency, it is most evident that it must be met and counteracted by a higher spiritual force and not by mere natural treatment.

And on the supposition that sickness is a divine discipline and chastening, it is still more evident that its removal must come not through mechanical or medical appliances, but through spiritual channels. It would be both ridiculous and vain for the arm of man to presume to wrest the chastening rod from the Father's hand by physical force or skill. The only way to avert God's stroke is to submit the spirit in penitence to His will and seek in humility and faith His forgiveness and relief.

From whatever side we look at disease, it becomes evident that its remedy must be found in God alone and the gospel of redemption.

Since disease is the result of the Fall, we may expect it to be embraced in the provisions of redemption. Therefore, we naturally will look for some intimation of a remedy in the preparatory dispensation to Christ's coming and the preaching of the gospel.

We are not disappointed. The great principle that God's care and providence embrace the temporal and physical as well as the spiritual needs of His people runs all through the Old Testament. Distinct provision for divine healing is made in all the ordinances of Moses. And the prophetic picture of the coming Deliverer is that of a great Physician as well as a glorious King and gracious Savior.

The healing of Abimelech, Miriam, Job, Naaman and Hezekiah; the case of the leper; the incident of the brazen serpent; the statute at Marah; the blessings and curses at Ebal and Gerizim; the terrible rebuke of Asa; the message of Psalm 103 and Chapter 53 of Isaiah—all leave the testimony of the Old Testament clear that the redemption of the body was the divine prerogative and purpose.

The Ministry of Christ

The personal ministry of Jesus Christ is the next great stage in the development of the principles of divine healing. In Christ's life on earth, we see a complete vision of what Christianity should be. From Jesus' words and works, we may surely gather the full plan of redemption. And what was the testimony of His life to physical healing? He went about their cities healing all manner of sickness and disease among the people. He healed all who had need of healing, "That it might be fulfilled which was spoken by Esaias the prophet, saying, Himself took our infirmities, and bare our sicknesses" (Matthew 8:17).

This was not an occasional incident. It was a chief part of Jesus' ministry. He began His work by healing the sick. He continued to heal to the close of His life. He healed on all occasions and in a great variety of cases. He healed without leaving any doubt or question of His will. He distinctly said to the doubting leper, "I will." He was only grieved when people hesitated to trust Him fully.

In all this Jesus was unfolding the real purpose of His great redemption and revealing His own unchanging character and love. He is still "the same yesterday, and to day, and for ever" (Hebrews 13:8). Surely we have a principle to rest our faith on as secure as the Rock of Ages.

Healing Is Centered in the Atonement

Redemption finds its center in the cross of our Lord Jesus Christ. There we must look for the fundamental principle of divine healing, which rests on Jesus' atoning sacrifice. This necessarily follows from the first principle we have stated: If sickness is the result of the Fall, it must be included in the atonement of Christ, which reaches as "far as the curse is found."

Peter states of Christ, "his own self bare our sins in his own body on the tree, . . . by whose stripes ye were healed" (1 Peter 2:24). In His own body He has borne all our bodily liabilities for sin, and our bodies are set free. In that one cruel "stripe" of His—for the word is singular—was summed up all the aches and pains of a suffering world. There is no longer need that we should suffer what Christ has sufficiently borne. Thus our healing becomes a great redemption right that we simply claim as our purchased inheritance through the blood of Christ's cross.

Beyond the Cross

But there is something higher even than the cross. It is the resurrection of our Lord. There the gospel of healing finds the fountain of its deepest life. The death of Christ destroys sin—the root of sickness. But it is the life of Jesus that supplies the source of health and life for our redeemed bodies. The body of Christ is the living fountain of all our vital strength. He who came forth from Joseph's tomb with the new physical life of the resurrection is the Head of His people for life and immortality.

Not for Himself alone did Jesus receive the power of an endless life. He received it as our life. God "gave him to be the head over all things to the church, which is his body" (Ephesians 1:22–23). "We are members of his body, of his flesh, and of his bones" (5:30). The risen and ascended Christ is the fountain of our strength and life. We eat His flesh and drink His blood. He dwells in us and we in Him. As He lives in the Father, so he who eats Him shall live by Him. This is the great, vital, precious principle of physical healing in the name of Jesus. It is "the life also of Jesus . . . made manifest in our mortal flesh" (2 Corinthians 4:11).

Healing Is New Life

It follows that this life must be wholly a new life. The death and resurrection of the Lord Jesus have made an infinite gulf between the present and the past of every redeemed person. Henceforth, "if any man be in Christ, he is a new creature: old things are passed away; behold, all things are become new" (2 Corinthians 5:17). The death of Jesus has slain our old self. The life of Jesus is the spring of our new life.

This is true also of our physical life. God does not restore the old natural strength. He does not build up our former constitution. We must let go of all the old dependencies. Our natural strength may fail. The life of Jesus is a strength that "out of weakness [is] made strong." It is a life that has no resources to start with. Creation-like, it is made out of nothing; resurrection-like, it comes out of the tomb and the failure of all previous hope and means.

This principle is of immense importance in the practical experience of healing. So long as we look for healing in the old natural life, we shall be disappointed. But when we cease to put confidence in the flesh and look only to Christ and His supernatural life in us for our strength of body as well as spirit, we shall find that we "can do all things through Christ which strengtheneth [us]."

It follows from this that the physical redemption that Christ brings is not merely healing but also life. It is not the readjustment of our life on the old basis, leaving it to go like a machine upon the natural plane. It is the imparting of a new kind of life and strength; therefore, it is as fully within the reach of people in health as those who are diseased. It is simply a higher kind of life—the turning of life's water into His heavenly wine.

It is only kept by constant abiding in Jesus and receiving from Him. It is not a permanent deposit but a constant dependence, a renewing of the inward man day by day. It is a strength that comes only as we need it and continues only while we dwell in Him.

A Sacred Life

Such a life is a very sacred thing. It gives a peculiar sanctity to every look, tone, act and movement of the body. We are living on the life of God, and we must live like Him and for Him. A body thus divinely quickened adds power to the soul and to all the service of the Christian life. Words spoken in this divine energy and works done through the life of God will be clothed with a positive effectiveness which must make others feel that our bodies as well as our spirits are indeed the very temple of the holy God.

The great Agent in bringing this new life into our life is the Holy Spirit. The redemption work of the Lord Jesus is not completed without His blessed ministry. Not as a visible physical presence does the Savior of sinners and of the diseased now meet the sick and halt and blind, but through the Spirit. All the old physical power is there. All the ancient results upon the suffering frame are produced, but the approach is spiritual, not physical.

The presence of Christ must be brought to our consciousness. But the contact of our need with His life must come through the Holy Spirit. So Mary had to learn in the very first moment of the resurrection. "Touch me not . . . I ascend." Thus, henceforth, must she know Him as the Ascended One. So Paul had ceased to know Christ Jesus "after the flesh."

Our Lord, when speaking to the disciples at Capernaum of the living Bread—the Source of healing—added: "What and if ye shall see the Son of man ascend up where he was before? It is the spirit that quickeneth; the flesh profiteth nothing" (John 6:62–63). This is the reason why many find it hard to meet the Healer. They do not know the Holy Spirit. They do not know God spiritually.

The sun in the heavens might as well be a ball of ice were it not for the atmosphere that attracts its warmth and light to us and diffuses them through our world. And Christ's life and love only reach us through the Holy Spirit, the Light, the Atmosphere, the divine Medium who brings and sheds abroad His life and light, His love and presence in our being. He takes of the things of Christ and shows them to us, extracting His life and sweetly diffusing it through every part of our being. He is the great Quickener.

It was through the Holy Spirit that the Lord cast out devils on earth. And now, "if the Spirit of him that raised up Jesus from the dead dwell in you, he that raised up Christ from the dead shall also quicken your mortal [body] by his Spirit that dwelleth in you" (Romans 8:11).

Free Grace . . .

This new life must come, like all the blessings of Christ's redemption, as the free grace of God, without works and without distinction of merit or respect of persons.

Everything that comes through Christ must come as grace. There can be no works mingled with justifying faith. So our healing must be wholly of God, or not of grace at all. If Christ heals, He must do it alone. This principle ought to settle the question of using "means" in connection with faith for healing. The natural and the spiritual, the earthly and the heavenly, the works of man and the grace of God cannot be mixed anymore than a person could expect to harness a tortoise with a locomotive. They cannot work together.

The gifts of the gospel are sovereign gifts. God can do the most difficult things for us Himself. But He does not help our self-sufficiency to do the easiest. A hopeless case is, therefore, much more hopeful than one where we think we can do something ourselves. We must venture on Him wholly.

If healing is to be sought by natural means, let us obtain all the best results of skill and experience. But if it is to be received through the name of Jesus, it must be by grace alone.

. . . Freely Given

It follows also in the same connection that if healing is a part of the gospel and a gift of Christ, it must be an impartial one, limited only by the great "whosoever" of the gospel. It is not a special gift of discriminating favoritism, but a great and common heritage of faith and obedience. It is "whosoever will, let him take the water of life freely." It is true that all who come must conform to the simple conditions of obedient faith. But these are impartial, without respect of persons and within the reach of all who trust and obey.

The simple condition of this great blessing—the condition of all the blessings of the gospel—is faith without sight. Grace without works and faith without sight must always go together as twin principles of the gospel. The one thing God asks from all who are to receive His grace is that they shall trust His simple Word. But this must be real trust. We must believe and doubt not. If God's Word be true at all, it is absolutely and utterly true.

With its living roots, a very small seed can split open great rocks and mountains, but the germ must be intact. One little laceration may kill its life. One doubt will destroy the efficacy of faith; therefore, it must begin by our taking God simply at His Word. A faith that is going to wait for signs and evidence will never be strong. Plants that begin by leaning will always need support. Indeed, the "faith" which rests upon seeing is not faith. "Blessed are they that have not seen, and yet have believed."

Abraham had to believe God and take the new name of faith and fatherhood before there was any indication of the answer. Indeed, every natural sign contradicted and stultified the promise. It is beautiful to notice the form of expression in Genesis 17. First Abraham was told, "Thou shalt be a father of many nations" (17:4). Then came the change of his name from Abram ("exalted father") to Abraham ("father of many"). It was the profession of his faith and the acknowledgment before a scorning world that he believed God.

Then follows God's next word. And how wonderful! The tense is changed. It is no longer a promise but an accomplished fact: "A father of many nations have I made thee" (17:5). Faith has turned the future into the past, and now God calls "things which are not" as though they were. (See 1 Corinthians 1:28.) So we must believe and receive the healing life of Jesus and all the blessings of the gospel.

More Than an Option

Are we under an obligation to seek divine healing of the body? Is it an optional matter with us how we shall be healed—whether we shall trust God or look to man?

Is this not "a statute and an ordinance" for us, too, and a matter of simple obedience? Is it not God's great prerogative to deal with the bodies He has redeemed, and an impertinence for us to choose some other way than His? Is not the gospel of salvation a commandment as well as a promise, and is not the gospel of healing of equal authority?

Has God not chosen to legislate about the way in which the plague of sin that has entered His world shall be dealt with? Have we any business to interfere with His great health promise? Has He not at enormous cost provided a remedy for the bodies of His children as part of His redemption, and is He not jealous for the honor and rights of His dear Son's name in this matter?

Does He not claim to be the Owner of His children's bodies, and does He not claim the right to care for them? Has He not left us one great prescription for disease, and is not any other course unauthorized and followed at our own risk? Surely these questions answer themselves. They leave but one course open to every child of God to whom He gives the light to see that His Word is "yea" and "amen."

God's Fixed Principles

The order of God's dealings with our souls and bodies is regulated by certain fixed principles. The Bible was written to state them in plain language for the wayfaring man. God works from within outward, beginning with our spiritual nature and then diffusing His life and power through our physical being.

Many persons come to God for healing whose spiritual life is wholly defective and wrong. God does not always refuse the healing. He begins in the depths of the soul, and when the soul is prepared to receive His life, He may begin to heal the body.

There is a close relation between the state of the soul and the body. John prays that Gaius "mayest prosper and be in health, even as thy soul prospereth" (3 John 2). A little cloud of sin upon the heart will leave a shadow upon the brain and nerves and a pressure upon the whole frame. A malicious breath of spiritual evil will poison the blood and depress the whole system. But a clear, calm and confident spirit will bring vigor into all the physical life. It will open the way for all the full pulses of the Lord's life in us.

Hence, also, healing will often be gradual in its development as the spiritual life grows and faith takes a firmer hold of Christ. The principle of the divine life, like the natural, is "first the blade, then the ear, after that the full corn in the ear." Many people want the head of wheat while the blade is yet tender. But it would only overwhelm us by its weight. We must have deep and quiet strength to sustain our higher blessing.

Sometimes this preparation is completed beforehand. Then God can work very rapidly. But in each case He knows the order and process best adapted to the development of the whole man. That is ever His great end in all His workings in us.

Some Limitations

Any limitations there may be of healing are also fixed by certain principles. Some enter not into this promised land because of unbelief and because they are a stiff-necked generation. Sometimes someone asks, "Why should people ever die if Christ will always heal?" Because faith can only go as far as God's promise, and God has nowhere promised that we shall never die during this dispensation. It is not immortal life that God promises in connection with the healing of the mortal body. The promise is fullness of life and health and strength up to the measure of our natural life and until our life work is done. True, it is the life of the resurrection that we have; but it is not the whole of it—only the firstfruits.

In speaking of our immortal life the apostle says: "Now he that hath wrought us for the selfsame thing is God, who also hath given unto us the earnest of the Spirit" (2 Corinthians 5:5). That is, as our earnest was a handful of the very soil of the purchased farm, but only a handful, so God has given us now by His Spirit in our new physical life a handful of the very life of the resurrection. But it is only a handful, and the fullness will not come until His coming. But that handful is worth more than all the soil of earth.

Shall we have strength for all kinds of supernatural exploits and extraordinary exertions? We have the promise of sufficient strength for all the will of God and all the service of Christ. But we shall have no strength for mere display and certainly none to waste in recklessness or spend in selfishness and sin.

Within the limits of our God-appointed work—and these limits may be very wide, much wider than any mere natural strength—we "can do all things through Christ which strengtheneth [us]." We may fearlessly undertake all labors, self-denials and difficulties in the face of exposure, weakness, conditions of climate and the most engrossing demands upon strength and time, where Christ clearly leads and calls us. We shall have His protecting power and find that "God is able to make all grace abound toward [us]; that [we], always having all sufficiency in all things, may abound to every good work" (2 Corinthians 9:8).

But let us touch the forbidden fruit, wander out of the sacred circle of His will or spend our strength on self or sin, and our life will lose its strength like Samson's arm and wither like Jonah's gourd. Yes, it must be true, always true, in our life as Paul says in Romans 11:36: "Of him, and through him, and to him, are all things: to whom be glory for ever. Amen."

CHAPTER

2

Divine Healing: A Hidden Treasure

By Peter N. Nanfelt

On a brief summer vacation in New Mexico, my wife and I spent a few days at a bed and breakfast outside the little town of Taos in the Sangre de Cristo mountains. Built three and one-half years ago in the adobe style, like so many buildings in that area, the five guest room establishment was attractive and well run. But according to the owner it wasn't easy to turn a profit in the competitive business of innkeeping, and except for an unexpected windfall, the bed and breakfast would have "gone under" before completing its third year of operation.

The owner told us she had owned a painting for sometime that she never thought was particularly attractive. When she built the bed and breakfast, she realized she needed something on a wall outside one of the guest rooms, so she hung the painting there hoping none of the guests would notice it.

But to her chagrin one guest did take particular notice of the painting and began to question her about it. The owner explained she knew it wasn't anything special and she had hung it there basically to fill an empty space on the wall. She was intrigued when the guest said, "Do you realize what you have hanging in your home?" She couldn't believe the implication that the painting she never thought to be particularly attractive might be of significant value.

Apparently an artist in California who did the piece a number of years before had become famous, and his paintings were in great demand. The owner of the bed and breakfast acted on the information she received from the helpful guest, did some research and eventually sold the painting for $75,000, enough to keep her business afloat until it had a chance to become profitable.

This is a classic and fascinating story about what we might call a hidden treasure—something of great value that was hanging in full view all the time but never taken seriously and never recognized as something that could bring help and hope.

In some ways the doctrine of healing is like that painting. The Christian and Missionary Alliance preaches what we have come to call the Fourfold Gospel. With the focus on Jesus Christ, we exalt Him as our Savior, Sanctifier, Healer and Coming King. We do not hesitate to lift up Jesus as the Savior of the world. Everyone who calls himself or herself a Christian, no matter the denominational background, proclaims this message.

The message of Christ our Sanctifier is somewhat more controversial in that there are differing beliefs about how the power of the Holy Spirit is experienced in the daily life of the Christian. We believe that Christ indwells us in the Person of the Holy Spirit and empowers us for life and service. While differences exist in the details of doctrine, the truth of the Holy Spirit and His ministry is proclaimed throughout the Christian Church worldwide.

The truth of Christ's return to earth as King is a teaching that is widely believed even by nominal Christians. The overwhelming majority of people in the United States profess to believe that Jesus will come back to earth. While for some reason this doctrine is not preached as frequently as it should be in Alliance churches, there generally is no hesitation to proclaim the reality of our Coming King.

The doctrine of Healing, on the other hand, remains the somewhat obscure aspect of the Fourfold Gospel. In some sense it is like a valuable treasure that has been there all the time but has gone unrecognized. As one who believes in the truth of Christ as Healer, it is not my responsibility, nor do I have the ability, to try and bolster the value and veracity of this doctrine. Christ needs no vindication or defense. His life and sacrifice for human need is of inestimable value. Nothing I nor anyone else can say will make this fact more or less true

Divine Healing: Why Doesn't Everyone Experience It?

As we all know, one of the major questions that has swirled around the teaching of divine healing is why, if it is a reality that Christ heals in answer to prayer, healings occur so infrequently, at least in the experience of most of us? And even if we have had the privilege of seeing many people healed, the question still persists: Why don't healings occur every time we pray for them?

It's an unanswerable question, of course. We have some ideas about this, and I'll offer a few momentarily, but the fact remains, no one knows why some people are healed while others are not. Indeed, ultimately there comes a time when each of us will die (if Jesus does not return first) so it is impossible to hold the view that Jesus' will is always to heal us. At some point His will is to call us home to be with Him.

There is clear evidence in Scripture, however, that at least on some occasions the reason healing does not occur is attributable to our lack of faith. The Gospels tell the story of the boy with the demon whom the disciples of Jesus could not heal. Jesus showed some exasperation with His followers and stated in no uncertain terms that they could not drive the demon out because they had such little faith (Matthew 17:20). We can only assume that this problem occurred on other occasions as well, given the slow learning curve of the disciples.

We also recall the depressing commentary about Jesus' ministry in His hometown. Matthew reports, "he did not do many miracles there because of their lack of faith" (Matthew 13:58).

On many other occasions Jesus indicated clearly that faith facilitated a person's healing. To the woman who had been subject to bleeding for twelve years and then was restored by Jesus' touch, Jesus said, "Daughter, your faith has healed you" (Luke 8:48).

James, who wrote one of the most definitive set of instructions for the Church regarding the ministry of healing, states clearly that it is the "prayer offered in faith" that makes the sick person well (James 5:15). He also talks about the importance of confessing our sins and the need for righteous living if we are going to experience the reality of Christ our Healer in our daily lives. So, while our focus is on Christ and He alone has the power to heal, we must be alert to the fact that we have a responsibility to live lives that will not hinder Christ's work.

But as indicated earlier, while strong faith is often a prerequisite for healing, it is not a guarantee that healing will occur. If it were, the basis of our healing would be our own faith rather than the Person of Jesus Christ. Sometimes we hear it said of people that they are relying on their faith to get them through a tragedy of some sort. Such a position is very precarious. Our hope and certainty is in Christ not in our faith! So while faith is often required for healing to occur, our faith does not heal—Jesus does!

At times we try to disguise our lack of faith by praying, "If it is Your will, please demonstrate Your healing power." This convenient little caveat often means we don't really believe God will answer our prayer for healing so we want to have in place a fallback position. That sort of "gamesmanship" may make us feel better, but it doesn't impress God.

But again, assuming our hearts are right with God and we are praying with the faith He has given us, we must ultimately conclude that God is in charge, and He will do as He wills. This would be a scary thought if our Lord was a pernicious, angry God bent on doing harm. Knowing that all He does is for our own good (Romans 8:28) makes it easy to accept the fact that sometimes our prayers for healing seemingly go unanswered.

Recently I was en route to Atlanta, Georgia, where I was scheduled to change planes and fly to Orlando, Florida. I missed the plane to Orlando because my flight into Atlanta was delayed for more than an hour. We were in the area but were forced to circle the airport time and time again. I never did find out if the delay was due to bad weather, excessive traffic or some other problem! But I had faith in the pilot to do the right thing. If I had any question about the pilot's ability, I wouldn't have been in the airplane to begin with. But I accepted the fact that he knew things I didn't know. It was my desire to land immediately so I could catch my flight to Orlando, a reasonable expectation. But I was more than happy to have the inconvenience of a missed connection so the pilot could get us on the ground safely.

When we pray for healing, sometimes for ourselves, sometimes for others, it seems so obvious to us what God's response should be. It is the reasonable thing for God to do. We are praying with clean hearts that are full of faith and He, after all, has promised to be the God who heals us (Exodus 15:26). But sometimes, often more frequently than we would like, He does not heal. In such cases we can only assume it is because He is privy to information we do not have, and while we don't understand what's happening, He is determined to do what's best for us. If we can accept the reality that ordinary people, like airline pilots, do things we don't understand but which we know are for our own good, can't we believe God to do that much?

Ultimately, the healing which Christ provides will be experienced in its fullness when we receive our heavenly bodies. As I mentioned earlier, even if we have enjoyed one or more experiences of divine healing, those healing experiences are only provisional since they eventually are canceled out by death, an inevitable reality for all of us. Some of us will know Christ's miraculous touch on our bodies here on earth, but *all* of us who have placed our faith in Him as our Savior and Lord, eventually will be given bodies that are imperishable, incorruptible and immortal. In that moment we will experience Christ's healing power in its fullness.

Divine Healing and Divine Health for Believers

It is not my intention in this chapter to provide an extended statement on the biblical basis for the doctrine of healing since the teaching will be clearly laid out by other contributing authors. What I want to touch on as a prelude to the primary thrust of this chapter, are the two most common ways believers experience Christ's healing provision in their lives.

As a family we look back on several experiences when God demonstrated His healing power in a very specific way. I remember an incident when, as young missionaries, my wife Jerry and I were on a trip in the interior of Kalimantan, Indonesia. We had been traveling by boat and by foot for four weeks, going from one village to the next, training believers and sharing the gospel in villages where there were no Christians. We were above the rapids and still had another day and a half trip which would take us back down the river through the rapids and on to our home. But Jerry fell seriously ill with dysentery and could not go on. We took refuge in a merchant's warehouse. As we tried to get comfortable for the night lying on burlap bags filled with various commodities, we cried out to God for Jerry's healing. Doctors and other medical help were several days travel by boat from our interior location. We were desperate. Suffice it to say, Jerry's healing was remarkable. The next morning we proceeded toward home without further delay.

More recently I was experiencing problems with my right eye, the eye in which I received a cornea transplant five or six years ago. It was constantly bloodshot and painful because on the surface of the eye there was a spot that was raised and causing irritation.

The doctor told me to wait for a week and if there was no improvement, he would need to scrape the eye. I later learned that this was a painful process that would probably put me out of commission for several days.

Five days went by and I didn't notice any improvement nor did I ask my colleagues at the National Office to pray for me. My reasoning was there were people on our team battling cancer and other life-threatening diseases. I had a little too much pride to ask prayer for a nonlife-threatening disease like mine.

Graciously, God spoke to me about this and I informed the staff, asking for their prayers. I had abandoned my contact lenses several days earlier and was wearing glasses, but after chapel that day I found my vision was seriously impaired using the glasses. I called my wife and asked her to drop off my contacts. When I put in the contact, I found I was able to wear it without difficulty. It was no surprise when the doctor told me the next morning that the raised area had disappeared, and there was nothing there to scrape.

When we speak of divine healing, we generally think of a personal experience or experiences that others have had, perhaps similar to those I have described where God's healing touch resolves a specific physical need in our lives. If we are living in the fullness of Christ and have committed ourselves fully to Him, we have the privilege of availing ourselves of this wonderful provision. It is a provision about which the prophet Isaiah spoke when he said, "Surely he took up our infirmities and carried our sorrows" (Isaiah 53:4). It would be natural for us of little faith to conjecture that Isaiah must have had something other than physical healing in mind when he made this statement. But Matthew clarifies Isaiah's comment with this incredible statement of his own: "When evening came, many who were demon-possessed were brought to him [Jesus], and he drove out the spirits with a word and healed all the sick. This was to fulfill what was spoken through the prophet Isaiah: 'He took up our infirmities and carried our diseases' " (Matthew 8:16, 17). Jesus is our Healer! He meets us at every point of our need, including our physical weakness.

While specific healings are perceived as the most dramatic demonstrations of God's healing power in our lives, we would be amiss not to recognize that the indwelling Christ provides strength for each day. As Dr. A.B. Simpson points out in his book *The Lord for the Body*, the apostle Paul is probably the best biblical example of a person who experienced the divine life of Jesus on a day-by-day basis. Reading of Paul's experiences in the Book of Acts, it becomes immediately apparent that he depended on Christ for each day's breath. In Second Corinthians 4:10 Paul writes, "Through suffering, these bodies of ours constantly share in the death of Jesus so that the life of Jesus may also be seen in our bodies." He goes on to say in verse 16, "Though our bodies are dying, our spirits are being renewed every day" (New Living Translation).

While we may have difficulty proving scientifically

that Christ provides strength and health for the believer on a day-by-day basis, such proof is irrelevant to those who have experienced Christ's enabling power.

In serving as a regional director and then as vice president for International Ministries for the Alliance, I traveled the world for nineteen years spending time in almost seventy countries. Some of the trips lasted as long as ten weeks. I was in and out of some of the least-developed countries and spent time in areas with some of the highest rates of malaria. During that time I had some colds and a few headaches but found it necessary to cancel my schedule and go to bed only one day in that entire nineteen years. I am not a particularly strong and robust person which makes it even easier for me to recognize the divine health I enjoyed.

When I became president of The Christian and Missionary Alliance, I asked God for physical as well as spiritual strength to carry the responsibility. At this writing it has been well over a year since I became president and except for the eye problem described earlier, I have been spared any illness—no colds, no flu, nothing.

I recognize there are undoubtedly other people, nonbelievers, who have also enjoyed good health during this period of time. But it is my personal conviction that, in my case, good health has been the direct result of the life of Christ demonstrated in my body. Not to recognize this aspect of divine healing is to miss an important and practical reality: Jesus not only provides healing for our sicknesses and infirmities, He provides good health for life and service. It is our delight, as believers, to avail ourselves of this blessing.

Divine Healing in Evangelistic Outreach

I come now to an aspect of healing that I believe should be in prominent focus as we enter a new millennium. Almost everything I've said so far relates the healing ministry of Christ to the believer. As I have indicated briefly using the passages from James, Isaiah and Matthew (and as other contributing authors will articulate more fully), there is a great deal of biblical evidence to show that, in a very special way, God provides healing for His people. It is clear in the Old Testament in the way that Jehovah cared for the Israelites, and it is clear in the New Testament where Christ the Healer takes center stage.

But the Bible is replete with examples of nonbelievers being healed as well. Strangely, we generally don't talk about this very much. When we have healing services they almost always are geared for believers. Our emphasis on the Lord for the Body is clearly intended to be a provision made for Christians. Our C&MA Council Healing Service usually is described as a "family time." I'm not suggesting this is inappropriate. These times of waiting on God as a group of believers are precious and very meaningful. We should have more of them!

But think with me about what took place in the Book of Acts. It seems that many of the healings (the miraculous signs) were done in an evangelistic venue. The apostles were empowered to do incredible things, almost on a daily basis, and these healings were used by God to bring people to salvation and faith in Christ. The experiences recorded in Acts and the ministry of Jesus reported in the Gospels shows that when God chooses, He heals nonbelievers as well as believers. It's possible, I suppose, to argue that everyone healed by Jesus and by the apostles came to faith before they were healed, but that seems to be unlikely.

Even if this was the case, the point I want to make here is that healings in the times of Jesus and during the development of the early Church were directly tied to the expansion of the kingdom. It also is interesting to note that almost all the healings mentioned in the first book of the Bible, and others which occur in subsequent Old Testament books, have to do with barrenness and are directly related to the holy lineage which produced the Messiah, the *Savior* of mankind.

The Book of Acts contains few examples of healings involving people who were clearly believers. Dorcas is identified as a "disciple" in chapter 9 (v. 36). Eutychus, the young man who fell from the window while Paul was preaching (20:1-12), could very well have been a believer also. Perhaps there are a few other such examples as well.

Evangelism, however, and the preaching of the kingdom of God were fueled by healings and other miraculous events. After Peter healed the beggar (3:1-10) he preached a powerful evangelistic message while he had the attention of the people. Following the death of Ananias and Sapphira recorded in Acts 5, it is reported that "The apostles performed many miraculous signs and wonders among the people. . . . More and more men and women believed in the Lord and were added to their number" (vs.12, 14). Acts 8:6 says, "When the crowds heard Philip and saw the miraculous signs he did, they all paid close attention to what he said." When Peter was in the town of Lydda (9:33-35) he healed a man who had been bedridden for eight years. His name was Aeneas. Verse 35 says, "All those who lived in Lydda and Sharon [a nearby town] saw him [Aeneas who had been healed] and turned to the Lord." In Acts 14:1-3 Luke writes about the ministry of Paul and Barnabas in Iconium saying, "So Paul and Barnabas spent considerable time there, speaking boldly for the Lord, who confirmed the message of his grace by enabling them to do miraculous signs and wonders" (v. 3).

In almost every instance in the Book of Acts where a healing is reported, the event is connected either directly or indirectly to proclamation. Even in the case of Dorcas' healing (a believer) Luke writes, "This became known all over Joppa, and many people believed in the Lord" (9:42).

The same pattern was true, of course, in Jesus' ministry. The more people who were healed, the more there were who believed. In a sense the healing ministry of Jesus was an evangelistic tool God used to expand His kingdom.

Before pursuing this further it is important to clarify that Jesus was compelled by compassion to relieve the suffering and hurt of mankind. Knowing what we do about the heart of God, it would be a gross error to suggest that neither Jesus nor the apostles, for that matter, healed people only to accomplish their evangelistic purposes in the world.

In our ministries of compassion, whether through CAMA Services overseas or through local endeavors in the inner city, we demean the Name of Christ if we offer help simply as a hook to bring people into the church. We help people in need because it is the right thing to do, and it is pleasing to God.

But it is even a greater error to minister to the physical needs of people while making no attempt to meet their spiritual needs. As I already indicated, public healings were almost always linked to proclamation in the New Testament. It is impossible to read the Gospels and the Book of Acts without being struck with this reality.

Another clarifying statement that needs to be made here is that God needs no vindication. Christ is who He is even if no one in the entire universe believes in Him. Christ did not need to do miracles to prove that He was God. He did not need to do mighty works through the apostles in order to earn His right to be the King. He did what He did out of compassion and because of His grace. Christ loved the world and was ready to do whatever He could to bring people to Himself.

I want to return now to our current experience in the Church of Christ in general and more particularly to our experience in The Christian and Missionary Alliance. Should the kind of healings among unbelievers that were so prevalent during the time of Jesus' ministry, and so evident during the development of the early Church, be a part of our ministry today? If not, why not?

First of all, I have heard people suggest that God may only chose to do dramatic healings, such as those recorded in the New Testament, among people who have little or no spiritual light. The evidence sighted for this view is the fact that in places where the gospel is being introduced for the first time there seems to be a much higher incidence of miraculous healings. In West Africa a number of years ago a French evangelist had a remarkable ministry with scores of verified healings taking place in conjunction with his campaigns. Our Alliance missionaries reported that virtually every person healed was a Muslim.

While the occurrence of numerous healings in non-Christian areas may lend credence to this view, the greater number of healings may more reasonably be attributed to the high level of evangelistic activity that is taking place in those areas.

If our primary ministries are carried out among the members of the Body of Christ, we give God little opportunity to use us to demonstrate His power among those who are unbelievers.

The second factor why we may be hesitant to involve ourselves in such ministry has to do with risk. Are we spiritually prepared to pray publicly for the healing of unsaved sinners? There will undoubtedly be brothers and sisters who will disagree, feeling that healing is reserved solely for those who are part of the Body of Christ. Perhaps the greater risk will be in praying for the healing of unbelievers knowing that such an effort could backfire if God doesn't see fit to heal. Christians who are not healed in answer to prayer generally have the spiritual maturity to understand some of the reasons why healing doesn't always take place, as I explained earlier in this chapter. This would not necessarily be the case with people who have little knowledge of God, possibly prompting them to ridicule God's servants who are attempting to be faithful to their evangelistic calling. Are we prepared for these kinds of encounters?

I can't help but wonder if the time hasn't come to take a new look at this kind of healing ministry. Even in our own country there are groups of people who have little understanding of the gospel. The secular mind-set, fueled by our educational system and the media, has produced a nation of "professing Christians" who have no understanding of what it means to enjoy an intimate relationship with a personal God. Maybe it will take evidences of God's divine power to move people toward Him.

I'm not sure at this point how we should proceed with such ministry. We not only have to deal with the doubt and sometimes the animosity of a secular population, we have to deal with the fact that we have been outflanked by the religious charlatans who have brought total disrepute on the Name of Christ and His healing power.

While these are legitimate concerns and while the risks are high, it would be tragic if God was withholding His power while waiting for us to make ourselves available for evangelistic healing ministries. As believers we take great comfort in the provision Jesus has made for the healing of our bodies and the restoration of our souls. We will continue to enjoy this gracious blessing of God as we live daily in His presence. But as we enter the twenty-first century and seek to be the people of God with a red hot passion for evangelism, will there be those from among our ranks who will have the courage of Peter and John to say to the sick and the needy, "Silver or gold I do not have, but what I have I give you. In the name of Jesus Christ of Nazareth, walk" (3:6).

CHAPTER 3

When Power Is Present

By James Davey

One day as he was teaching, Pharisees and teachers of the law, who had come from every village of Galilee and from Judea and Jerusalem, were sitting there. And the power of the Lord was present for him to heal the sick. Some men came carrying a paralytic on a mat and tried to take him into the house to lay him before Jesus. When they could not find a way to do this because of the crowd, they went up on the roof and lowered him on his mat through the tiles into the middle of the crowd, right in front of Jesus.

When Jesus saw their faith, he said, "Friend, your sins are forgiven."

The Pharisees and the teachers of the law began thinking to themselves, "Who is this fellow who speaks blasphemy? Who can forgive sins but God alone?"

Jesus knew what they were thinking and asked, "Why are you thinking these things in your hearts? Which is easier: to say, 'Your sins are forgiven,' or to say, 'Get up and walk?' But that you may know that the Son of Man has authority on earth to for-

give sins. . . ." He said to the paralyzed man, "I tell you, get up, take your mat and go home." Immediately he stood up in front of them, took what he had been lying on and went home praising God. Everyone was amazed and gave praise to God. They were filled with awe and said, "We have seen remarkable things today." (Luke 5:17-26)

I'd like you to recreate this scene in your minds. Picture what the Scripture has just described. Take a mental snapshot. What do you have in your picture?

Certainly you have the Lord Jesus Christ; He is at the center. He's in command of every scene in which He makes an entrance. You have the Pharisees; they are the antagonists. The Pharisees are never on the side of the angels. They are strict in their observance of the law; orthodox in their interpretation but are consistently wrong-headed.

You have four men. You wouldn't know that from this text but Mark tells us there were four who brought the paralytic to Jesus. And of course you have the paralyzed man! He's the cause of all this activity. He is one of those for whom Jesus Christ has come.

There is poignant symbolism in his illness. He is paralyzed; he is helpless. That's the human condition without God, and that's our condition apart from God. Unable to make our own way; not beyond help, but helpless.

I hope you're building this scene in your mind with me. Do you see anything else? Oh, you see a Palestinian house made of mud bricks with roof tiles laid across wooden beams. But is that all? No there's a crowd there, so we fit the crowd into our picture. And that's it.

But if that's all you see, you're not seeing enough. You need to look again and look more deeply. What do we have here this morning? We have a crowd of people, the participants, this room. But the most important element is invisible, just as in the scene we have been recreating from Luke 5. It is the most important observation of all and it is found in verse 17, when Luke records "And the power of the Lord was present for him to heal the sick."

"Power was present!" That's the only reason this scene is memorable and the only reason it is recorded for us. Power was present! Does that mean that sometimes power was absent in the life of Jesus? That's a new thought, but the answer is "absolutely, yes."

Applause but No Faith

Nazareth was an example of that. The Scripture says that in Nazareth He "could do no mighty deeds." Nazareth is a good example of a predicament we sometimes find ourselves in, for in Nazareth Jesus was present but no mighty deeds were done. In describing our Lord's visit to Nazareth Luke 4 says, rather surprisingly, that "all spoke well of Him." Everyone in Nazareth was pleased that He was present. They applauded Him. Isn't that ironic? They spoke well of Him, but no mighty deeds were done!

Mark 6 attributes the results in Nazareth to a lack of faith. As a consequence the power of the Lord was absent. I wonder how many places there are today in our nation where people will speak well of Jesus, but no mighty miracles will be done . . . no mighty works . . . no lives changed . . . no sense of the presence of God . . . no sense of the glory of God . . . no awareness of His power. Oh, good things are done and wonderful things are said and good deeds are performed, but there are no mighty, earthshaking acts of His power.

There are churches that can only be characterized as powerless and helpless. Oh, nice, good things are said about Jesus, all across our country. Nothing bad will be said about Him, but when all is said and done, more will be said than done!

We sometimes fall into the trap of thinking that our greatest spiritual enemy is outright opposition. We talk a lot about the persecuted church. I would not for a moment minimize that suffering. But we do need to remind ourselves that often the places where the church is growing the fastest are the very places where there is opposition.

We talk about a cold, secular, humanistic world; about a culture in which we find ourselves that is alien to God's grace. As if that were our greatest enemy. But the greatest hindrance is a lukewarm church where Jesus is well spoken of, but no mighty deeds are done. What the church needs, and what we need as we head back to our homes and ministries, is a fresh realization that the power of the Lord is present!

When the power of the Lord is present, it doesn't much matter what else is or isn't present. Early in my ministry I had four wonderful years at the Northside Church of the Alliance in Pittsburgh, now known as the Allegheny Center Alliance Church. We met in an ancient building 130 years old. The sand bricks had long been weakened by decades of rain and wind. In the center of that sanctuary hung a huge iron chandelier from an intricately vaulted ceiling that noticeably sagged. I can remember sitting on the platform thinking to myself, "I don't want to be here when that lets go!"

The square back boxed pews would never pass the comfort test. There was no narthex in the church, no place for people to gather before church or after. The old organ wheezed as it was played. It was old: In fact it was the oldest pipe organ west of the Allegheny Mountains. While I was there urban renewal came to the North Side of Pittsburgh. It looked like Belgrade after a NATO raid. One street after another was ripped up. Every building in the neighborhood was torn down. Once multi-story buildings ringed the church. Now there were holes in the ground where rubble lay.

There was no off-street parking. Oh, there was one lot that might hold about a dozen cars but that was all. But in spite of all the physical deficiencies three times each Sunday that church was crowded to capacity with 600-700 people in every service. Week after week people met God in that place because the power of the Lord was present.

What is the power of the Lord?

Last Christmas in my Advent preaching I got stuck on the name Emmanuel—God with us. I had come through a long and sometimes difficult year with many stresses. I can remember meditating on the name and asking myself, "Is He with us now? Is He an 'is' or is He just a 'was'? Is He with us in this church now? Or can we only say, 'He was with us, in a former day and in another place.' " You see, the implications of that are enormous.

That kicked off for me a reading and rereading of the four Gospels to discover what I could about what Jesus said about the Holy Spirit for I instinctively knew that the power of the Lord was the power of the Holy Spirit.

I first read the Gospel of Mark. Mark was almost certainly the first Gospel written, sometimes called the Memoirs of Peter. I was amazed to find that in Mark there are virtually no references to the Holy Spirit. The Holy Spirit was invisible in Mark's Gospel, being mentioned in only two places, His baptism and His warning against the blasphemy against the Holy Spirit. That's it. That's the sum total . That's why I say the Holy Spirit is invisible in Mark.

Then I read Matthew. Matthew is very likely the second written account of Jesus. Matthew goes into considerably more detail than does Mark. And in the Gospel of Matthew I found the Holy Spirit is only incidental. There are a few references to the Holy Spirit but He is not central. He is not a major theme. He is mentioned in the birth narratives at the beginning of Matthew and in the Great Commission at the end of Matthew in addition to what Mark gave and that's it. That's Matthew. Only incidental.

Then I read Luke. Luke was written as an apologetic. Luke said he had investigated everything and was setting out to write an orderly account. What I found in Luke is that the Holy Spirit is instrumental. He is the instrument by whom and through whom God works. To be sure much of the same material is in Luke as I found in Mark and Matthew but with a difference.

In Luke 4:14 we have a verse that illuminates several other later statements. We read that "Jesus returned to Galilee in the power of the Spirit." Not in

His own power, but in the power of the Holy Spirit. It was the power that had come upon Him at His baptism. Then we have our text this morning in 5:17 that says "the power of the Lord was present to enable him to heal."

In 6:19 we read that "power was coming from him and healing them all." In 8:46 we read Jesus said, "Someone touched me; I know that power has gone out from me." There's one more reference in Luke's Gospel and it's important for us to understand because it tells us that this power is transferable. It is in 9:1-2 where Jesus called the Twelve together and "he gave them power and authority . . . and . . . sent them out."

In Luke we see that the Spirit is the power by whom Jesus carried out His ministry, His miracles, His teaching. The magnetic drawing appeal of His person was the Holy Spirit. It wasn't something about His appearance, it wasn't His piercing eyes, it wasn't some mannerism. It was simply the power of the Holy Spirit. More importantly, He conveyed that power to the disciples when they went on assignment.

Of course there's one more Gospel, and that's the Gospel of John. You already know what I found in the Gospel of John. The Holy Spirit is simply inescapable in John. In chapter after chapter we are confronted with the presence and the power of the Holy Spirit. The rich tapestry of our Lord's teaching about the Holy Spirit is found in the Gospel of John. Almost half the chapters in John's Gospel mention the Holy Spirit.

The Inescapable Holy Spirit

Now let me make three simple observations and try to tie them back to our text that says that "the power of the Lord was present . . . to heal." The first observation is how differently the four Gospels treat the Holy Spirit. It is very striking. I read Mark and He is invisible. In Matthew He is incidental. In Luke He is instrumental and in John He is inescapable. There He is everywhere present. Four Gospel writers, each of them recording the same life that they in common hold to be the life of God come to earth, yet each of them treats the Holy Spirit in a different way.

Now there's no great moral or theological significance to that, but I did puzzle over it until I realized that the Gospels form a kind of mirror by which I can see myself. The reality is that in some churches the Holy Spirit is invisible; present but not recognized. In some churches the Holy Spirit is incidental, treated much like the creed treats Him. The Apostle's Creed says "I believe in God the Father, Almighty . . . and in Jesus Christ, God's only Son." Then there's a great deal about Jesus. Near the end of the creed there's this statement, "I believe in the Holy Ghost." Without any further elaboration the creed simply moves on to other truths. He seems almost incidental.

Yet in other churches the Holy Spirit is instrumental. What I mean is that there is an expectancy that the Holy Spirit will show up. That He will be on time. That He will do His mighty work. Thank God in a few places dotted across our world the Holy Spirit is found as He is in the Gospel of John, everywhere present, working mightily to do His will. There you cannot escape the awesome sense of the presence and the power of the Holy Spirit. There are places you cannot explain apart from the fact that God is at work and His power is being shown; places where we can only say, as does our text, "and the power of the Lord was present." Everyone of us pastors wishes that could be said of our church.

More Books, Less Power

The second observation is that Jesus said little about the Holy Spirit. Taken in the context of the four Gospels; relatively little. What He said, of course, is life-changing. But I typed out every word that Jesus said about the Holy Spirit and found I had far less than two pages of typescript. That's not much at all. In 1894 A.B. Simpson, our founder, undertook a study of the Holy Spirit at the Old Orchard camp meeting. That fall in New York City he expanded on that series from his pulpit. Later the studies were put in book form, which we have in the classic volume *The Holy Spirit*, or *Power from on High*. Stephen Merritt, in the preface to Simpson's book, noted the the absence of literature about the Holy Spirit and in a rather quaint way said, "the book of the Holy Ghost has yet to be written." That was 1894. In the 106 years since then, many books have been written about the Holy Spirit, and if we could pile them up, I think they might reach from the floor to the ceiling. We have more books but not necessarily more power.

One reason the Holy Spirit is not given a prominent place in the Gospels is that He is the enabler. For example in John 14, Jesus said, "[the Holy Spirit] will teach you all things and will remind you of everything I have said to you." In the next chapter, John 15, Jesus said, "[the Holy Spirit] will testify about me." In John 16, Jesus said, "He will bring glory to me by taking from what is mine and making it known to you." So the role of the Holy Spirit is to magnify Jesus Christ, to make Him real, to exalt Him.

One measure then, of how well we know the Holy Spirit, and how complete our surrender to Him may be, is how much we talk about Jesus Christ and how close and personal is our relationship to Jesus Christ. The measure is not how much we talk about the Holy Spirit, but how well we know Jesus Christ. To please the Holy Spirit we focus on Jesus, because that's what He does. So when we say the power of the Lord is present, we are saying the Holy Spirit is present, and He is essentially hidden, invisible, known only by the consequence of His activity.

Much to our chagrin and often totally unrelated to our preparedness, or the excellence of our programs or the fever of our activity, we come to discover that "the power of the Lord is present" at times when we are not expectant.

Trouble Indicates the Spirit Too!

The third observation is that the presence of trouble is no evidence of the absence of the Holy Spirit. This was most startling of all to me. In John 14 Jesus gave His exposition of the Holy Spirit in the context of betrayal and denial and opposition and trouble and persecution and hatred. The promise of the Holy Spirit was clearly set against the disciples' bereavement and loss and loneliness. In effect Jesus told His disciples, "Yes, I'm going away, but I am going to send the Holy Spirit to counter your fear and anxiety."

These two themes are simply woven together in these three chapters of John's Gospel, 14, 15 and 16: The presence of trouble and the presence of the

Holy Spirit. Now this is counter-intuitive. You don't come to this conclusion by natural thought processes. Our minds tell us that if there is trouble God is absent, and if there is peace God must be present. That's intuitive thinking.

What makes this utterly striking is that by and large we equate success and popularity with the blessing of God and we equate prosperity and "results" with the mighty power of God. We see a church succeeding in its ministry and conclude that God is mightily at work there. Now if I understand this correctly, the Holy Spirit can be just as real, just as present, just as personal, just as powerful when everything is going wrong. Success is not by itself a reliable indicator that the Holy Spirit is present in power.

I think of our missionaries who for decades went to Cambodia, lived their lives there, preached the gospel, shared the good news about Jesus Christ and saw at best a handful of converts. Today we know Cambodia is a rich and fruitful field for the gospel of Jesus Christ. Does that mean that now the power of God is there and that before He was not present? No, not at all. It took a huge amount of the power of God just to keep those missionaries in Cambodia and let them live out their lives there so that today another generation could see the harvest.

You may be in a troublesome period in your life. You may be a trouble-filled church, whether pastor or layman. You may be tempted to think God has forsaken you, that you are overwhelmed by sorrow and loneliness. Weakness and fear and anxiety may have the upper hand.

But I want to tell you that you have not been forsaken or forgotten. The Holy Spirit is the specialist given to comfort and strengthen and sustain you in tough times.

Armed with the Power

The question is not whether you and I will go home to happy and successful and growing churches. Some will and some won't. The question is will we go home to churches armed with the power of God's Holy Spirit. Are we described and defined by Luke 5:17 that says "the power of the Lord was present . . ." or by Mark 6:5 which says "He could not do any miracles there."

It doesn't really matter now how we came to this Council; how beaten up we were, how close we were to calling it quits. Whatever level of disappointment or desperation we registered on Tuesday night is by now irrelevant.

What matters is that we go home to our churches in the power of the Holy Spirit. What matters is that we stand in our pulpits not with something good to say, but with Someone to say through us what He wants. What matters is that we confront the powers of darkness, face the army of critics and stare down every obstacle because the power of the Lord is present!

I want to tell you a story about my friend Jerome Jackson, who is pastor of the Alliance church in Largo, Florida. It's actually about his daughter Sandy and her baby. When Sandy was five months pregnant she went to see her physician. It was on January 8. She received both good news and bad news. The good news was that she was carrying a baby girl. The bad news was that there was a chromosomal abnormality. It was devasting.

The doctors told her the baby had no cerebellum so there could be no brain development. There was a malformed heart without a left ventricle and no septum on the left side. There was evidence of an indented skull, bulging eyes from hydrocephaly, nasal bone and nostril deformities, a pear-shaped abdomen, a calcified liver, a kidney cyst, a cleft palate, one clubbed foot and deformities on both hands.

This Family Doesn't Do Abortions

As compassionately as he could the doctor advised them to seek a therapeutic abortion. To this Sandy quietly said, "Doctor, this family doesn't do abortions."

But the reality of the baby's condition remained. There was much prayer, many tears, days of fasting and prayer, crying out to God. Their pride was utterly set aside as they wept before the Lord. And as incongruous as it seems, at one point during all this, Sandy was given a vision by God of standing before the congregation on Mother's Day cradling in her arms a perfect, beautiful baby daughter.

On April 22 a decision was made to induce labor, about two weeks early. A neonatologist was called in to consult, a team of doctors was at the ready to resuscitate the baby as necessary.

First the skull presented itself. It was round, beautiful and covered with reddish hair. Then the face, perfectly formed with a cute little button nose. Then the rest of her body. The hands and feet were no longer deformed as was seen in utero. Her lungs filled with air and as she let out her first cry Grandma Jackson looked inside her mouth and exclaimed, "Sandy, there's no cleft palate."

By this time the delivery room had turned into a revival meeting. Praises filled the air and they realized they were on holy ground. The power of the Lord was present to heal!

Over the next four days every test known to medical science was performed on Rebecca. Specialists were brought in from all over South Florida. Every square inch of her little body was examined and the assumption seemed to be that "there must be something wrong with this baby!"

And yes, two weeks ago on Mother's Day, Sandy stood in her church cradling a perfectly beautiful baby Rebecca. Now I have told you that story in order to get to Sandy's comments. She wrote, "For the rest of our lives we want to testify to the miracle God has done for us. God is so good." And then this line which has been ringing in my heart for the last month since I first read it. "Whatever you are facing in your life right now, rest assured that He is bigger than any problem you will ever have."

The power of the Lord is still present and as He sends you and me on assignment He will give His power and authority.

CHAPTER 4

Christ My Healer, My Life

By Alfred C. Snead

During student days at Nyack I was walking down the hill one day with Rev. Kenneth MacKenzie, a member of the faculty. The conversation turned to Christ's healing ministries, and Dr. MacKenzie said, "Young man, it is one thing to know Christ as Healer; it is another thing to know Him as your life."

So real did this precious lesson become in the years that followed that, while rejoicing in the privilege of testifying to the healing power of Christ, I found a deep joy in the realization that this healing virtue is but a part of the vital life-flow which the risen Christ desires to have revealed by the Holy Spirit in the members of His Body.

Within a few months after arriving in India as a young missionary in 1907, I was stricken with tuberculosis of the lungs and soon began to suffer severe and frequent hemorrhages, even though I continued to be active in language study and in work as assistant treasurer of the Mission.

One day I had occasion to go from Dholka to Kaira in Gujarat with some visiting missionaries.

While there my condition became worse, and Miss Eunice Wells and other missionaries and Indian women workers of the Kaira Girls School and Orphanage met in a little room to pray for my recovery. During this prayer meeting the Holy Spirit witnessed that I would recover, but no manifestation of healing was given.

Later that afternoon I traveled by two-wheeled horse cart to Mehmedabad, then by train to Ahmedabad. After crossing the city to Sabarmati, I waited several hours for the train to Dholka, arriving there after midnight. There I was met by a missionary colleague, Rev. John Culver, and we traveled by camel to the mission station on the outskirts of Dholka.

During the trip on the train I was involved in a continual fight of faith, even though often I longed to succumb to the weakness and give up the battle. Nevertheless, throughout the testing the Lord gave witness that He would honor the deep yearning of faith and love that I might be spared for service for Christ.

During the next twenty-four hours I suffered four severe hemorrhages. The first ceased after earnest prayer by Mr. Culver and myself, but the second continued despite our prayers until other workers were called to join in intercession. The third persisted even though the same group gathered again and word was sent out to others on the mission compound to unite in prayer.

Some hours later a fourth hemorrhage, the most severe of all, seemed to be draining the last of my life blood, and answer to prayer was not manifest until all activity ceased in the orphanage, schoolroom, shops and the Bible school, and both adults and children gave themselves to prayer. Then God answered and the hemorrhages ceased, never to be repeated.

Great Physical Weakness

Nevertheless, I continued to experience great physical weakness. While at a minor hill station, Chikalda, during the next hot season, two medical missionaries of the Free Church of Scotland, each the head of a mission hospital, asked permission to examine me. I was told that my left lung was practically useless and that my death warrant would be sealed if I remained in India six months longer. Even if I returned to America, my one hope of life was to go to the mountains. If I lived there and became strong enough after five years, I might do light work such as keeping chickens. But I was told I could never hope to preach or teach again. Much prayer was offered, but God did not heal me in India.

Upon arrival in the United States I was not financially able to go to the mountains. Mrs. Snead and I lived in Indiana with my parents.

In those days the Alliance Board gave no allowance to those not in active service, and soon I had to seek such employment as my weakened condition would permit. Thus circumstances all combined to make it necessary to depend upon God alone for life and strength, for healing and help.

Many friends joined with us in earnest prayer for my recovery, and God answered. After little more than a year had elapsed, I passed a rigid physical examination before Mrs. Snead and I joined the staff at the Wilson Memorial Academy at Nyack. Not only the local physician but the State Board of Health in Indiana certified that I was free from tuberculosis.

The Lord's grace has abounded in giving me strength as my day.

While preparing for a trip to the Far East in 1940 to confer with workers in eight Alliance fields, God gave me various portions from His Word to encourage me. The presence and providences of God were marvelously real each step of the way and the entire trip was made without any serious delays, despite the restrictions caused by the wars between Japan and China and between French Indochina and Thailand, and the resultant cautions and censorship which were evident in every place I visited in those Far Eastern lands.

The first severe physical test came during the six days of horseback travel from Lanchow, Kansu, over the mountains to our mission stations in the interior of West China. While traveling sometimes through snowstorms and at altitudes ranging from 9,000 to 13,000 feet, I began to suffer intensely in my heart and would frequently have to dismount and rest or ride in a Chinese chair borne on the shoulders of two coolies. But this also caused great physical distress.

After three days of travel we had a day and a half of fellowship, rest and service in Hochow, a great Chinese and Muslim center. Three days more brought us to Hehtsuh, a Tibetan center at 11,000 feet.

The morning after our arrival the missionary men and I went up a hill to call on the Living Buddha, the spiritual head not only of the monastery of 300 Tibetan Buddhist priests, but also tens of thousands of Tibetans in the district. After calling on and presenting New Testaments to this man and other officials in the monastery, we had breakfast with two Tibetan priests to whom we also gave Testaments.

That afternoon I was quietly reading in Isaiah and praying in my room in the mission house, amid great weakness and some suffering. Suddenly two hands seemed to be placed upon my chest and something took place which brought me instant deliverance. I had no heart trouble during the following days.

Later, after traveling over snow-covered roads in the mountains, through deep dust in the valleys and waiting in the chill dampness of early winter in Lanchow for the arrival of the plane to take me to Chunking and thence to Hong Kong, I contracted a very severe cold, coughing frequently through the days and nights.

Trouble with one of the motors held the plane overnight in Chengtu. There I stayed in a cold Chinese hotel and later spent hours out at the airfield waiting for clear weather. The coughing continued and was somewhat aggravated by the necessity to spend about six hours on two successive days at the open airport on an island in the Yangtze River.

A Quiet Assurance

While in Hong Kong preparing for my travel to French Indochina and other fields, I had little time for rest and the cough grew worse. On my first Sunday in Vietnam, Rev. E.F. Irwin, the chairman, said to me, "You surely cannot preach this evening, can you, Brother Snead? You have been coughing most of the time night and day during the three days I have been with you."

I replied, "Are the people expecting me to preach?"

He said, "Oh, yes, you have been announced to preach tonight."

The Lord gave me quiet assurance in my heart that He would undertake and I said, "Yes, Brother Irwin, I will preach tonight. The Lord has never let me down yet."

That night as I preached in the Tourane church, filled to overflowing with Annamese Christians, missionaries and others, God gave the victory. Missionaries told me my voice was never clearer, and I have had no cough from that night in December 1940 to this present hour. Blessed be the name of the Lord. Hallelujah!

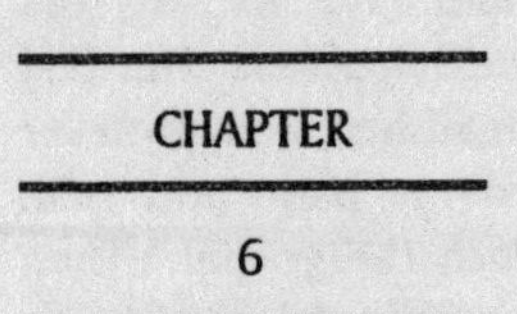

By Way of the Valley of the Shadow of Death

By William G. Weston

My story dates back to 1881 when a humble Christian mother dedicated my life to God before I was born, and received a revelation from the Lord that someday I would be an ambassador for Christ and in His stead beseech men to be reconciled to God.

From that time she never doubted, and though she went to be with the Lord without seeing her vision fulfilled, she died happy in the faith that what God had promised He was faithful to perform.

As I write this testimony my heart marvels at the grace of God, and I rejoice with joy unspeakable and am full of glory as I see the hand of God guiding, directing and leading me to the place where I could say, "Not my will any longer, Lord, but Thine alone. Bless His dear name."

I was saved in an old-fashioned meeting at the age of ten years, and Jesus was very real to my heart. As I grew older and rebelled against God's plan for my life as He had revealed it to my mother, I grew cold in my heart toward the things of God and entered into a business career determined to have the things of the world, and live my life as I desired. My mother was always sweet and patient with me, and when opportunity arose she would remind me that at sometime God would have His way, and then alone would I know true happiness. Her last words as she lay upon her deathbed, I shall never forget, as she smiled, patted my hand and said: "Someday, Billy, you will preach the gospel." Then death claimed her body and she slipped away to be with Jesus, leaving me in God's hands.

Through the years that followed, the struggles and heartaches were many, but the hand of God was upon my life, and goodness and mercy followed me, although I confess at times I did not recognize them.

At the close of the first World War, I returned home to my family and again entered the business world. The conviction was strong within me that I should yield my life fully and let God have supreme control, but when I thought of my family, my own unfitness for the ministry and all the mountains which stood in my way, my heart failed me. I compromised my convictions and decided to remain in business where I was prospering, and pour money into God's treasury so that others who were prepared could go forth with the gospel message. However, I was to learn through sad experience that when God wants your life, He does not want your money as a substitute.

The strain of the months which followed resulted in a physical collapse from which I was a constant sufferer until God in His mercy met me almost five years later.

My break came suddenly, although I received many warnings which I passed unheeded. One Sunday morning I awakened with distress in the region of my heart, but went ahead with my duties as Sunday School Superintendent, hoping it would pass away. The distress, however, increased. I attempted to walk home but collapsed on the road with a violent heart attack which lasted for fifteen hours. During that time my faithful family physician never left me. It seemed that my life would surely go out, but God spared me and finally my heart calmed down, but left me in a pitiful condition. My nervous system collapsed, and one organ after another failed to function due to the lack of nerve stimulation.

I had the best attention and care medical science could offer, and I am very grateful for all that was done for me during the years of my sickness. At times it seemed I was on the way to recovery, then I would suffer another relapse. I was treated in the hospitals and clinics, as well as by private physicians and specialists. When drugs were finally taken from me I tried osteopathic and chiropractic treatments, in fact everything that held out any hope for my recovery, but they all failed. Finally I was discharged from the hospital and sent south to die.

At this time my heart was in such a condition that my physicians told me they did not know how I had lived as long as I had. My stomach had failed and I could not digest food without the aid of digestive fluids. My lower bowel was paralyzed and my whole body emaciated. I weighed only 123 pounds. My eyes were failing fast and I suffered from violent headaches due to the dying nerves.

I arrived in Miami, Florida, in January 1926, traveling by boat from Baltimore, Maryland, in the care of a companion. I was located in that beautiful city with all the comforts of life, but they meant but little in my hopeless condition. I had said good-bye to all I held dear on earth and had nothing to look forward to but death. It seemed as though I was forsaken—that I had surely come to the end of myself. All the things I had counted on had failed.

Then my chance came. Lying on my bed on a Sunday morning, I looked over the church page of the newspaper and there before my eyes was the advertisement, "Old Time Revival, 33rd Street and 5th Avenue." Immediately there came into my heart the strong desire to be taken there. I spoke to my companion, who reluctantly agreed to accompany me. That was how I came to attend my first Christian and Missionary Alliance meeting.

There was a large audience present that Sunday evening, and my heart was blessed by the inspirational singing, and the simple gospel message which was preached to the unsaved, resulting in a good number going forward for salvation. Then the messenger, Rev. Raymond T. Richey, looking over the audience, made this statement, "If there is someone here tonight sick unto death who cannot find healing, if you are God's child and believe His Word, you can be healed in your body just as you were saved."

It seemed that message was for me alone. Yet it seemed too good to be true, as I had been taught that the days of miracles were past, that when doctors failed there was no further help. I was greatly agitated in mind, and asked to be taken to my room so I could think the matter over.

There were banners on the walls of the Tabernacle bearing the following Scriptures:

> Jesus Christ the same yesterday, and to day, and for ever. (Hebrews 13:8, KJV)

> Who forgiveth all thine iniquities; who healeth all thy diseases. (Psalm 103:3, KJV)

> That it might be fulfilled which was spoken by Esaias the prophet, saying, Himself took our infirmities, and bare our sicknesses. (Matthew 8:17, KJV)

When I reached my room I took my mother's Bible and searched the Scriptures and found them just as in the Tabernacle. Oh, how God began to talk to my heart! During the period that followed I daily studied the Word until my heart was convinced that Jesus was still able and willing to meet all who came to Him in faith. So I was led to return to the meetings at 10 o'clock in the mornings, as I was stronger then and did not suffer so much pain as later in the day.

I was not healed at once, but my heart was encouraged by the Word of life and the testimonies of those who had met God. My heart began to trust as the blessed Holy Spirit ministered to me.

It was about two weeks after my first visit, following several mornings of refreshing, that I was carried once more, like the lame man of Acts 3, to the Beautiful Gate. That was the day when I was to receive more than I expected.

I was sitting near the front of the church waiting for the service to open, when a stranger came to me with this greeting.

"The Lord led me to come to you as I am in great trouble and need someone to stand with me in prayer."

I looked up and answered, "Friend, you have company, for I am in trouble too."

Then he poured out his heart, telling me of his

wife who was paralyzed on one side, of the little children who needed a mother's care and of the struggle they had passed through until their money was exhausted yet no help had come. Now that they had spent their all, they had come to the place of prayer. If God did not heal her they were hopeless.

My heart was greatly moved as I listened. I realized that God was my only hope so I covenanted with this stranger to pray. As the meeting opened, we all bowed our heads and sought God's blessing upon the service. For the moment I forgot my own need and began to pour my heart out for my brother. And, behold, as I prayed for another, heaven opened *to me*, Jesus was revealed to my heart as the Healer divine, and Matthew 8:17 became a living reality. As I worshiped Him, life flowed through my body from my head to my feet, and I was like the woman who touched His garment. I felt in my body I was healed. Oh, glorious day! I cannot tell you with what words I praised my Lord. I only know my cup ran over, and I gave glory to God as the Holy Spirit fell upon the people assembled, about 1,000 in number. Many were saved, filled with the Holy Spirit and healed. What a joy it was to see my new-found friend coming forward with his wife. Her arm that had been paralyzed was raised to heaven and she too was whole.

I left that service a new man, and from that hour every organ of my body has functioned properly. I have had the joy of giving my redeemed body to my Lord, who filled it with His blessed Spirit, and I have had seventeen years of service, preaching throughout the United States and Canada, enjoying marvelous health, weighing 210 pounds as I stand before the people, an example of God's grace and faithfulness in answer to a mother's prayers.

What He has done for me He will do for you, beloved, because Christ tasted death for every man and "whosoever will may come." Will you not yield and trust my Jesus? He will not disappoint you. God bless you real good!

CHAPTER 6

My Face Was Eaten with Cancer

By H.P. Rankin

I was born at Mountain City, Tennessee, December 26, 1905. However, I do not remember much about the Tennessee mountains, as my father moved to Spotsylvania County, Virginia, a few miles from the city of Richmond, when I was four years of age. I was one of eleven children, and we were very happy on the farm until some of the older ones began to seek employment in the city and elsewhere. At the age of sixteen I quit school and went to Spruce, West Virginia, to work for the West Virginia Pulp and Paper Company. I worked there for a year or so and then went back to Richmond and started to work for my brother-in-law as a carpenter's helper.

During this time I began to attend The Christian and Missionary Alliance Church in Richmond and gave my heart to the Lord Jesus Christ. Everything went well for about two years, until I was forced to go back home in the country, because of the lack of work. There I started with the "old gang," and after sometime drifted away from God, back into sin more than ever before. I had joined the church when I was twelve years of age and was baptized, but I am sorry to say I did not know the first thing about salvation. As I began to go to all kinds of worldly places, the thought of God and His work vanished from my mind.

Back home I was able to secure work with a large grocery company, and in six weeks was promoted to the position of manager of one of their stores. God began to speak to me again about my soul and my promise to live for Him. However, it seemed that the voice of conviction drove me further from the Lord. I would go out in sin at night and come home and be miserable, knowing that I was lost, without God or hope in the world. Nevertheless, the things of the world had me surrounded. I was not willing to let go and let God have His way. After about four years of this kind of work I was ready for a change. I secured work with the Dupont Rayon Company of Richmond and was given a very responsible place.

I thought I was all fixed for life, with money coming in as never before, a position that I knew would last and nothing to worry about. However, my folks began to pray that the Lord would save my soul. They would go to church and I would go out for a night of sin. As they prayed I became miserable but would not listen to God. Later the folks at the Alliance Church began to pray that the Lord would save me regardless of the cost. I knew something was going to happen. I had a desire to come to the Lord but did not have the power within myself to make the change and would not confess my sins before God or man.

In the fall of 1931 I contracted sarcoma cancer in the left cheek. I was sent to the best doctors and hospitals. At one time I had a capsule of radium in my face valued at $50,000.00, along with seven radium needles. I had several hemorrhages and lost so much blood that I became so weak I could hardly lift my head. Still determined to have my own way, I would not surrender to the Lord.

Then one day I was taken from the hospital with no hope of ever recovering. But God's people continued to pray. Some would pray all night that I would give my heart to Christ and that He would heal my body. Frankly, I was disappointed with preachers. Some would come to my home and pray for me, and then tell the folks that it was only a matter of time, that it was impossible for me ever to be a well man again.

At about that time the Lord sent a young minister to our city, and well do I remember the first words that I heard him speak: "A cancer is no more in the sight of God than a cut thumb. There is nothing too hard for the Lord Jesus Christ. 'Himself took our infirmities and bare our sicknesses.' 'I am the LORD that healeth thee!' "

These words came from the young pastor of The Christian and Missionary Alliance Church in Richmond, Virginia, as he sat beside my bed Sunday afternoon October 15, 1933. However, they were just so many words to me. I had been given up to die by some of the best cancer doctors in the South. I had been under constant medical treatment for about eighteen months. I had been in the hospital for x-ray, radium and electrical treatments, but I continued to grow worse, until the doctor told my wife and family that there was absolutely no hope for my recovery. They said the cancer had eaten away the greater part of my cheek bone. When I would rinse my mouth, I would wash out pieces of bone as thick as a match stick, and sometimes one-half inch long. Two back teeth had been eaten away. However, the doctor said that he was willing to try to get me into a certain cancer hospital in one of the Midwestern states. With my consent he wrote the hospital explaining the case, and immediately the following letter came back, which I now have in my possession:

> Dear Doctor,
>
> Your letter of September 30th in regard to treatment for case with cancer in the upper maxillary was received today. We do not advise the ______ treatment in bone condition; therefore feel that it would be unwise for you to attempt so serious a condition. It is better, doctor, if you can pick your case, to begin with a more simple case.

After receiving this letter, the doctor came again, and this time with nothing to offer or even suggest. He said they had done all that was humanly possible to do. By this time I had been examined by several noted physicians. They had not considered expense in the case; now they were at the end of themselves. All that they could do was to give me more codeine and morphine, along with the four aspirin tablets that I was taking every two hours, day and night, to keep me in a semiconscious condition. As the pain grew more severe, the amount was increased.

Naturally, being an unsaved man, those words of the minister about healing sounded absolutely absurd to me. Yet he seemed so positive in his conviction that before he had left my room I had begun to think about life throughout eternity. Where would I spend eternity? I knew only too well; and I began to search for this Jesus that the minister of the church and some of the members had been telling me about. How He would forgive if we would confess our sins, and bring peace to a troubled heart.

Truly, before I was taken sick I enjoyed the pleasures of this world, as most sinners do, but now the things of this life could do me no good. I craved something better. I knew that the pleasures of this life are gratifying, but never satisfying. By this time there was an empty, hollow place in my heart and life that the things of the world could not fill. On Sunday, October 22, 1933, I came to the Lord Jesus Christ as a poor, cancer-eaten, miserable, lost sinner. There on my bed, at the cross, I surrendered my life unconditionally to HIM. He saved me from my sins. PRAISE HIS HOLY NAME! He touched my body, and put a joy into my heart and a new song into my mouth, and sent me on my way rejoicing.

I began to study His Word in order to know His will, that I might please Him in every way. Through the reading of His Word (the Bible) and fellowship with Christians, I began to grow both spiritually and physically, and by January 1934, I was able to attend the services at The Christian and Missionary Alliance Church in Richmond; and there at the altar, January 6, 1934, I was anointed by Rev. W.G. Weston and the pastor of the church, according to James 5:14-16, and the Lord Jesus Christ marvelously healed me. At that time I weighed about 128 pounds; in less than three months I weighed 170 pounds, which I have retained until the present time. I gained this weight at a rate of from two-and-one-half to four pounds each week.

I did not feel any great change in my life that night at the altar before God; but the next morning about 4 o'clock I definitely received the baptism of the Holy Ghost in my life. There in my bedroom He came into my life, and praise God, He has been very real to me ever since. Oh, the joy that came into my home! My wife who, had been a Christian for sometime, was praising God that He had saved my soul and healed by body. My little daughter who was only four years old at that time was so happy as she went about telling her little friends that her "daddy was going to get well again." The doctor who had not seen me for sometime could not understand what had taken place when he saw the inside of my mouth. The cancer had eaten a hole in the roof of my mouth about the size of a fifty-cent piece, the flesh around the hole had decayed, but now had fallen off and had left nothing but pure clean flesh with no sign of the old cancer. Nevertheless, the doctor wanted me to let him insert radium again to be sure the trouble would not return, as he said he knew the healing was only temporary and that I could not possibly live. "Cancers," he said, "do not get well that way."

In the summer of 1934 the Lord called us out into full-time service. Feeling the need of training, we knew we were to go to the Missionary Training Institute at Nyack, New York. But how? Every available dollar had gone for doctor and hospital bills. But the Master was saying, "GO," and "Lo, I am with you alway, even unto the end of the world" (Matthew 28:20, KJV). We arrived at Nyack September 6, 1934. After registering for the fall semester, we had only $20.00 left, my wife, my little girl and myself—with no means in the natural to make our way; but we still had the promise that He gave us—"Fear not . . . be glad and rejoice: for the LORD will do great things" (Joel 2:21). God marvelously supplied our every need until graduating from school in 1938.

Truly, the Lord has done great things for us whereof we are thankful—supplied our every need, spiritually, physically and financially. After leaving school we served as pastor of The Christian and Missionary Alliance Church, South Richmond, Virginia, for sixteen months, after which time we were called as pastor of The Christian and Missionary Alliance Church, Durham, North Carolina. Since coming to Durham almost four years ago, we have been very busy in His work, speaking on an average seven times each week since August 1939. God has given us a daily radio program over station WDNC here in Durham, broadcasting a fifteen-minute program four days each week. God has signally blessed this radio work. Many souls have been saved. Several have been healed. Believers have been strengthened in the faith. Several have written in to tell us that they heard the truth concerning the Second Coming of Christ for the first time over our broadcast. How we do praise the Lord for the privilege of working for Him in these last days.

CHAPTER 7

Six Out of a Hundred

By V.R. Edman

For every believer whose home going antedates the rapture of the saints at the Second Coming of the Lord Jesus Christ, there comes the moment to die. Just what are the sensations peculiar to that mystic moment is a personal matter peculiar to each individual? From biography we have learned the experiences of some of God's people who have been conscious until the last, and have been able to express something of their feeling and understanding of the last moments of earthly existence. What others who were unconscious to the world about them thought and felt, we of course cannot know. As far as I had any degree of consciousness or understanding I had come to the last moments of this life one Saturday evening late in June of 1925. I remember distinctly having the thought, *Now I am about to die.* The rapturous, exotic thought of one's seeing the Savior within a brief moment or two is beyond description and has no place in this narrative.

High in the Andes Mountains of Ecuador I contracted typhus fever. After the annual missionary conference in the fall of 1924, Mrs. Edman and I settled in the mountain city of Riobamba, which lies in the great valley between the two ranges of the Andes, at an elevation of 9,000 feet above sea level. The work of the gospel faced much hostile opposition in that area, and was a good proving ground for young missionaries. The powers of darkness pressed heavily against one's spirit, and there were few reasons for encouragement apart from the promises of God.

On May 15, 1925, our first son, Charles Raymond, was born. Several weeks later I went to Indian villages lying high above Riobamba to oversee the property of a mission station of the Gospel Missionary Union, which for the time being was without a resident missionary. At the time there was considerable illness among the Indians into whose houses I went, looking for property which had been stolen from the mission house. Afterward, on the long road down the mountain into the valley, I was aware of a general pain throughout my body which made it necessary for me to dismount occasionally from the horse and to lie prostrate by the side of the road.

On arrival home I was seized with a tremendous chill. Hot coffee, warm soup and even walking in the sun-drenched patio in the heat of the day did not seem to bring any warmth. Intuitively, I knew I was ill, but thought the chill would pass by the morrow.

On the following morning, which was Sunday, I was able to make preparations for a small morning service being held in our living room. Chairs were put into place and hymnbooks distributed in anticipation of the coming of a few believers and others interested in the Sunday morning gospel service. (The afternoon and evening of the Lord's Day were devoted to tract distribution and open-air work.) Before anyone arrived, I sat down by the little folding organ and played a few melodies for my own heart's good. I played through the first stanza of "Anywhere with Jesus I Can Safely Go," and was beginning the second stanza when a terrific pain in my head caused me to be so blinded that I could not continue playing. I was able to stagger somewhat uncertainly to a room in the rear of the patio and to lie down on a cot, after instructing Mrs. Edman to care for the morning service.

Now I knew I was ill and felt that the disease might be of a contagious nature, so I instructed Mrs. Edman and the little native girl in the home that I was to be left alone as much as possible. There was no one in the city who had much concern about the foreign missionary and not until nearly a week had elapsed did one young physician come for a brief visit to the home. He informed Mrs. Edman that he thought the disease was paratyphoid and later he changed the diagnosis to typhoid fever.

Later in the week after I lost consciousness during the day and the night because of the high fever, Rev. George P. Simmonds, then a missionary of The Christian and Missionary Alliance and for the time being on special service for the American Bible Society, came to our home. He had been in Peru for several months and was en route to his home in Quito. It took him only a moment to diagnose the urgency of the situation. In the providence of God he had met an official of the Guayaquil and Quito Railway on the train that day. When Rev. Simmonds applied to the local agent in Riobamba to transport a sick missionary in the baggage car of the train leaving early the next morning for Guayaquil, he was refused. But with persistence he insisted on calling his newly met friend by long distance telephone. The headquarters of the railway in turn called the local agent to instruct him to have the baggage car unloaded of all non-fragile materials and to make space for the patient. A gang of Indians was occupied all night in that task.

Very early on Saturday morning I was sufficiently conscious to note that I was being carried by some Indians from the home to the station. Now and then I recalled some word from Rev. Simmonds or noticed the ice provided by station agents who had received a request from him for the same. In the evening of that day we reached the end of the train journey, and we were received by a delegation of missionaries and native Christians, among whom I recognized Rev. W.E. Reed, the chairman, Rev. John D. Clark and Rev. Roscoe O. Stull, who had recently arrived on the field. They carried me through the streets of Guayaquil to the clinic of Dr. Baker, an American physician and long a resident of Guayaquil.

From that point onward I have little recollection of events except for two or three. I do remember Dr. Parker's coming into the room for just a brief moment. Later I learned from Rev. Reed that the physician just walked in, took a glance and walked out with the comment, "He has typhus, and has been too long without treatment in the high altitude. At best, only six out of a hundred live through typhus." It was late that evening when I had the distinct impression that the moment to die had now come.

Others would have to fill the details of the subsequent days. Mrs. Edman came to Guayaquil on the next train which arrived on Tuesday, to learn that her husband was very low and possibly not expected to live. On the next morning she came to the clinic, only to be refused admission to my room on the ground that her husband was already dead, or at the best, about to die. She insisted upon being admitted to the room, and has told me that the native nurse sadly pointed her distracted attention to the extremely weakened condition of the patient and that already his feet were cold with death. In some manner she found her way to the mission house where much prayer had been made, but where now preparations were asked by the physician for the funeral service. It is the law in Guayaquil that because of the heat of the tropics, a corpse must be buried on the day of death unless the demise occurs very late in the afternoon, in which case the funeral can be held early in the morning. Someone helped Mrs. Edman dye the only dress she had, which was her wedding dress. Rev. W.E. Reed, the chairman, made the appropriate preparation with an undertaker because Dr. Parker said, "This man cannot live until noon."

On his way from his sad duties, Rev. Reed stopped at the infirmary to learn from the doctor that the patient was still alive, but with only the faintest spark of life remaining. The good doctor was not conscious of the fact that at that time the Spirit of God had laid a great burden of prayer on hearts far and wide. Missionaries and Indian converts in Agato, where I had first labored in the gospel, had given themselves to prayer. The Summer Convention at Camp Hebron near Attleboro, Massachusetts, was in session. The leader, Rev. E. Joseph Evans, then District Superintendent of the Alliance in New England, interrupted the regular session to call for prayer. There are many friends in New England who bear witness that they will never forget the urgency and agony of prayer offered for several hours, until prayer had been turned into praise. They began to know that the effectual, fervent prayer of a righteous man had availed much and that the prayer of faith had saved the sick. Thirty-five hundred miles away, and beyond the equator, their intercession before the Throne of Grace was answered; life lingered all that day and the night following. On the morrow Dr. Parker asserted, "If the patient can hold out for forty-eight hours more, there is hope." Because I write these words, by way of testimony, you can know that he lived through the forty-eight hours, and now for many years after that.

Consciousness returned very slowly. I do recall faintly hearing one of the nurses say that, "Today is Dr. Parker's holiday." Possibly she meant it was the fourth of July. Nearly a week later I remember beginning to recognize Mrs. Edman but could not tell who accompanied her, despite the fact that they were fellow missionaries, some of whom had been fellow students with us at Nyack. The first clear recollection was the celebration of Bastille Day (July 14) when there was a local celebration in honor of the French national holiday.

Some weeks later I was removed to the mission home where more than a month was spent in recovering sufficient strength to walk to and fro and read the Bible for just a few moments at a time. Strength returned gradually and steadily.

Over the years I have had protracted seasons of very hard and exacting work in the service of the Savior, but there have been strength and joy to perform the same. Withal there is the consciousness of working on borrowed time, for the goodness of the

Lord to raise one from the depths of the valley of the shadow of death can only mean to go on in His glad service. I am one of the "six out of a hundred."

His ways are higher than our ways as heaven is high above the earth. For no merit or worthiness on my part has the span of life been extended. Its time and strength must be devoted to the Task Worth-while.

CHAPTER 8

My God Can Do Anything

By Clarence Shrier

Shortly after her vacation with the children, my wife had a heart attack and her doctor informed us that she needed an extended rest. That meant that she and the children would have to go to my wife's parents' home and I would have to go to the sanitorium. It seemed to be the only way my wife could get the rest she needed.

And yet that wasn't what the Lord had promised us. He had promised us that He would keep our family together and that nothing would separate us. We wanted that.

So after the doctor went, my wife came to my room and kneeled beside my bed. We knew nothing about healing, but that day we prayed with a passion because we didn't want to see our little family separated. We knew that God had put us together and we felt that He wanted us to remain together.

And that day as we prayed, God reached down and instantaneously healed my wife. When the doctor came the next morning, he found her on her knees scrubbing the floor. She has never had any sign of a heart condition from that day to this. Oh, I don't know what your God can do, but I know what my God can do!

The Bible says, "He healeth all diseases," and no truer words were ever spoken. For Jesus has never gone back on His word. What He has promised He is able to perform. He performed a miracle in her life that day and it remains today.

And yet not all healing comes that quickly. I was a T.B. victim for years. There were times during my years of sickness when I got so hungry to go to the house of the Lord that my wife would help me out of bed, bathe me, clothe me and have some of the men come and carry me to the car. When I arrived at the church they would carry me up the steps and place me in a special chair that was prepared for me at the back of the church.

I'll never forget the first time I went like that: As they were lifting me out of the car, my pastor was coming down the street and as I looked up, he raised his hand in the air and said, "Welcome home, brother Shrier!" And when he said that, the tears began to stream down my cheeks because it gave me just a taste of heaven. I foresaw the day when I would arrive in the presence of the living God and He would life up His arms and say, "Welcome home, welcome home!"

Oh, sometimes I really hungered to go to the house of God, because I delighted to be with the Lord's people. I believe that when we are born again of the Spirit of God we'll delight in the Word of God, we'll delight in prayer, we'll delight in the fellowship of the saints. We will know that we are one in Christ and that we are all purchased by the precious blood of the Christ who was a Lamb without blemish and without spot.

In 1945 I came down with tuberculosis of the bowel, and for the next three years I lived on pablum and cod-liver oil. I couldn't even take as much as a full swallow of water because of the intense pain, nor could I take milk of any kind because it would spread the disease. I don't know if you've ever lived on pablum and cod-liver oil or not, but it certainly isn't a steak diet!

In 1948 I was called into the Queen Alexandra Sanitorium, where my doctor asked me to take a seat in his office. He said, "Clarence, we'd like to take seven ribs out of each side."

I asked, "Doc, what good will it do?"

"Well," he said, "it won't do too much good, but you'll be able to sit around for a few years and enjoy life. I'm going to be perfectly honest with you. We are not going to operate on you, because if we were to operate on you with that tubercular bowel condition you wouldn't last over two months. You will have to stay and have your routine checkup."

That night the nurse came into my sanitorium room with some castor oil for me. If you know anything about that type of tubercular bowel you can imagine what castor oil would do to it. And whatever you imagine, it happened to me!

I took that castor oil, and my bowel began to roll and my fever started to rise. I looked at the bed next to me and what I saw was discomforting. I saw a young lad who was dying of a tubercular bowel. There was nothing but a skeleton under those covers. He hardly made a wrinkle in the bed. He had to have a plug in his rectum to keep the juices from flowing out, and when they pulled the plug you either had to crawl out or get wheeled out or walk out because of the stench of his rotting bowels. (Incidentally, that young man was later miraculously healed in answer to the prayers of God's people.)

But when I looked at him that night, he was a dying victim with practically no hope. And in him I saw myself. Not liking what I saw, I turned my face to the wall about midnight and prayed until about 2 o'clock in the morning.

At 2 o'clock that morning I felt the hand of God placed on my side. Out of the tips of the fingers on that hand there seemed to be electric current going forth and spreading all through my bowel. My bowel stopped rolling and my fever went down and I went to sleep. I didn't even have a bowel movement.

When I was taken downstairs the next morning to be examined the technician could only shake his head in amazement. "What's the matter?" I asked.

"I don't know," he replied. "I can't understand what's taken place here. You have the bowel of a new-born babe. You'd better go up and tell the doctor." So I headed my wheelchair toward the doctor's office to do just that. And before I got there the technician phoned the doctor and gave him the report.

So the doctor was expecting me. When I arrived, he said, "Well, now I can have the seven ribs out of each side!"

"No you can't doc. I'm going home! If God can do what He has done, He can do even more." And so I was taken home. But I was put to bed, because although God had healed my bowel I was still strictly a bed patient.

The following Sunday afternoon I asked my wife to leave me for awhile because I had a great desire to pray. I prayed for approximately three hours. God gave me five promises for my lungs. Then I called my wife back into my room and I told her what the Lord had done and I asked her if she would call her employer to ask him to call his nephew, the head doctor in another sanitorium nearby. I wanted to make arrangements for another x-ray the following day.

After her employer had made the arrangements, they took me to the sanitorium the next day. There they took x-rays of my lungs. When the doctor checked those x-rays, he found that I was healed completely in my right lung, and healed up to the apex in my left lung. After coming from the dark room he said, "I can't understand this! Why wasn't the apex healed?"

"I don't know, doctor," I replied. "I don't understand it anymore than you do, but would you call my doctor in London and relate the news?" That he did.

I went to London the following day and was informed that they were going to take three ribs from my left side. My brother from Badaxe, Michigan, came over to see me and when He came into my room, he discovered that I was so full of joy and peace, and that my countenance was, as he said, so "radiant," that he turned on me and said, "How can you be like that? Don't you know that you could die while you are under the anaesthetic? Don't you know that this is a serious operation?"

And I said, "I know, but my heart is full of joy and I can't react in any other way!" And he actually became so panicky that he left that room and never returned. He couldn't understand how anyone could have such peace and joy in the midst of a crisis.

Well, I was wheeled into the operating room and the next day three ribs were taken out of my left side. The next morning I awoke with a bag of pellets pressing my apex down.

That day I turned on my radio and there was Ed

McEwen singing the gospel of Jesus Christ. I blended my cracked voice with his, and at the sound of my singing, lights began to flick on all over the hallway. The nurses wondered why everyone had gotten sick at the same time! Well, they hadn't. They were just wondering about that crazy guy at the end of the hall who was singing at the top of his one lung!

Three weeks later I was again wheeled into the operating room and three more ribs were taken from my left side. The operation was in the muscle-and-nerve area and the pain of such an operation is usually so intense that a patient requires hypodermic injections every four hours for at least four days. I have seen patients on those "hypos" ten days.

But after my operation as I reached around and touched my back, there was no pain at all. My wife was visiting at the time and I said, "Honey, have I been operated on?" And when she assured me that the operation really had been performed, I said, "I can't believe it, because I haven't got a single sore spot or pain!"

The nurse came in to give me a hypo. I had no pain whatever, but she insisted on giving me the hypo because it had been ordered by the doctor. So she gave me the hypo and I got so sick she had to call the doctor from the operating room. When he came in he said, "What's the matter with you?"

I said, "I don't know, but I don't need the hypos. Please take them off the book."

He replied, "Well, I'm not going to take them off the book, but I am going to instruct them to give you hypos only as you ask for them."

As the days slipped by, I never had to ask for a single hypo, because I never had another ache or pain. Oh, God not only bore upon Himself my sicknesses; He also took upon Himself my pain.

As I was recuperating there in the sanitorium and waiting for my stitches to be removed, I got to know some nurses from the London Bible Institute who worked at the sanitorium at night. They would come to my room at the end of their rounds and we would have a little cup of tea and a word of prayer, and the they would go on their way.

One night as I was waiting for them to come into my room and take care of me for the night, a light appeared on the wall. Call it a dream, call it a vision, call it what you like, but I was there and that light was as large as the noonday sun. And as I looked into that light all I could see was a shadow.

The shadow began to take form. Wasn't I terrified? No, as I lay there watching I was wonderfully wrapped in God's peace. Never had I been in a place of such serenity! The quietness of heaven had settled upon my sanitorium room.

And as I lay there looking into that light I heard a voice. It was God's voice. And in an unforgettable, audible voice God spoke to me these words: "Go and stand and speak in the temple to the people all the words of this life."

I took my first deep breath in ten years. I said, "I'll go anywhere You want me to go."

When the nurses came in that night I told them what had happened. Did they get excited! They stayed all night to see the doctor when he arrived the next morning. And as soon as he came in, they told him about it and he came up to my room and said, "What's happened to you now?"

"I don't know," I said. "But I think I've been healed."

We'll find out," he said.

They examined me nineteen times in the next three weeks and couldn't find a thing. Finally, they released me. When the doctor told me I could go home I said, "How do I get there? By train or by car or by ambulance?"

"Anyway you can get there," he answered. "As far as we know, you're the first case in medical history that has been released from the surgical floor without his ribs."

My charge nurse came and said that she would drive me home. To get me ready, they took a sponge-like ball and placed it on the outside of my body where my ribs had been taken out; then they pulled it tight with three-inch tapes so that I would have some support. I was ready to go!

But when I tried to get out of bed a sudden pain struck me in the back as if someone had stabbed me with a knife!

I knew what it was. It was a pinched nerve. And I also knew it was a trick of the devil. So I grabbed the side of my mattress and pulled myself up as perspiration literally dripped from my chin. Once out of bed, I somehow got into my robe and my slippers.

I got my shoulder against the wall and I said, "I'm going, Lord. I'm going out of here no matter if it costs me my life. I know this is a trick of the devil and I'm not going to give in to him."

And I started to walk out. Oh, how it hurt! When I got into the hall, I had my shoulder against the wall and I was still all bent over. How the nurses stared at me! They couldn't believe their eyes! But I kept pressing on, using the wall as my support.

And suddenly the pain lifted and I was free. I went back to my room and took off my robe and my pajamas and put on my clothes and rode sixty-five miles home. I've been going ever since. I don't know what your God can do, but I know what my God can do. Anything!

Divine Healing and Demon Possession

By Keith M. Bailey

For too long church theologians have looked upon the exorcising of evil spirits as a relic of a primitive mentality which modern development and knowledge have conquered. Modern Satan worship, spiritism and the popularity of astrology have brought a new awareness of paganism in North America; shock waves from the movie "The Exorcist" are still with us.

The truth is that demons do exist and do enter and control human personalities. The validity of the exorcist, however, is often confused with the credibility of divine healing. Both exorcism and divine healing have been misunderstood by people predominantly influenced by naturalism and humanism.

Any interpretation of divine truth must be tested by principles of understanding which support a total view of divine revelation as found in the Scriptures. Sin has darkened the understanding of man and the powers of evil exercise pernicious influence on the conscious mental life of people. Wherever Satan and demonic activity are exposed, here confusion and distortion will be prevalent unless strong counteraction is taken.

The Naturalist Mentality

Naturalism is not of modern origin; it began with Adam and Eve in the Garden of Eden when Satan said: "You surely shall not die! For God knows that in the day you eat from it your eyes will be opened, and you will be like God, knowing good and evil" (Genesis 3:4-5). Naturalism asserts that man can take a position independent from God and can determine good from evil for himself.

The Greek philosophers five centuries before Christ believed that they could discover ultimate reality and whatever gods there were. According to modern naturalism, we can know only that which can be proved with our senses or with scientific data; the universe is confined to that which we observe by using the discoverable laws of cause and effect.

Though this philosophy is not explicitly taught openly, its presuppositions are generally assumed in the modern classroom and in various media.

Christians do believe in the uniformity of natural laws, but to them the cosmos is not a closed system and God cannot be confined in it. In the long run, Christianity alone makes technology possible, in terms of its view of an ordered universe and all that is implied. It is not incidental that modern technology developed after the Renaissance and the Reformation.

There are two parts to reality; beyond the natural world there is a supernatural universe of both good and evil. There is an evil spirit world with power to enter man who volitionally invites such spirits; but beyond this, there is a heaven where love, goodness and ultimate and absolute truth dwell with the eternal God.

The Christian is called upon to demonstrate in history that the supernatural world exists, particularly that God not only exists but that He is both immanent and transcendent. Secularism is the refusal to let God be God. It denies the relevance of Christianity to the major concerns of life and preoccupies itself with interests other than loyalty to God and warfare against Satan and his spirits.

The Need to Understand Demonology

The modern scene calls for a fresh look at biblical demonology as it relates to the everyday life and ministry of the church. For many years evangelical Christians have been willing to accept the fact of demon possession in pagan cultures, but have been almost totally unaware of the presence and work of evil spirits in Christian nations.

The devil is smart enough to adapt stratagems to the enlightenment of the age, but changes that have come about in the culture of the twentieth century are such that demonism is now as prevalent in the so-called Christian countries as in many non-Christian countries. It seems incredible that witchcraft, sorcery, divination, astrology and other forms of mediumistic contact with evil spirits should be so widely practiced in Western civilization, but anyone who is knowledgeable of Western culture today knows that demonism is enjoying an enormous revival. It is estimated that there are at least four hundred full-time spiritists in New York City alone.

This increase in demonism is a natural result of

the basic philosophy of humanism and naturalism that has governed man's thinking in much of the Western world in the last hundred years. Because of the vacuum that results when man becomes his own god, he has little alternative but to turn back to the devil. He begins to worship the powers of darkness and to seek the supernatural through this medium rather than to recognize the supernatural power of the true creator God.

Not too many years ago theologians were questioning whether or not demonism was actually a reality. Even those who were somewhat conservative in their theological position were of the opinion that Christ may have been compromising at this point with the ignorance of His day. That He looked upon mental disorder and psychological problems as the work and activity of evil spirits.

An inductive study of the New Testament Scripture disproves this position. Christ clearly made a distinction between mental illness and demon possession. The phenomena and activity of demon possession were explicitly given in the New Testament Scriptures.

It is important that the church restudy her doctrine and also her practice with regard to the phenomena of demon possession. Although a great rarity a few years ago, now pastors, elders, Sunday school workers and youth workers are constantly encountering what apparently are strong cases of oppression and, in many instances, actual possession. Anyone who has an extensive ministry in today's culture needs a working knowledge of biblical demonology and the biblical practice of exorcism. He may have no need greater than the ability to recognize the devices of Satan.

Defining Exorcism as Distinct from Healing

Exorcism and healing are not one and the same thing. They are closely related, and both rest upon the finished work of Christ and the authority invested in the church through the name of the Lord Jesus Christ. When Jesus sent out the twelve, He "gave them power and authority over all the demons, and to heal diseases" (Luke 9:1). The same Scriptures that authorize the church to heal authorize the church to also cast out spirits in the name of the Lord Jesus (Mark 16:17-18; Acts 8:7; 16:8; 19:11-12).

Church history shows that in ancient times the church practiced exorcism extensively. In the third century when most of the church's converts were from paganism, it was common practice that an exorcist would minister to the new converts alongside the catechist. One would teach them Christian doctrine, the other would deal with any existing ground for the possession and activity of evil spirits in their lives. Prior to their baptism, converts were not only taught doctrine but were thoroughly delivered from every vestige of their worship and devotion to the evil spirits. When infant baptism was first practiced, the catechumen's preparatory acts were combined into the liturgy of baptism and exorcism became an integral part of the rite.

Before exploring the biblical teachings of the practice of exorcism the reader should have in mind a clear definition of demon possession. It is only fair to say that there are mental and nervous disorders that are not demon possession. Unfortunately, extreme viewpoints have been held by some, indicating that all mental illness has an evil spirit at its source. Mental illness could be due to some physical disorder or some weakness and, therefore, cannot necessarily be attributed to an evil spirit.

Christ is able to heal mental illness just as He is able to heal physical illness. It is appropriate to anoint and pray for the mentally ill that they may recover. Remarkable incidents can be cited of healings in answer to pray for those with mental and nervous disorders.

Demon possession is a condition that may have the outward appearance of mental disturbance and nervous disorder, but the activity of a personal evil spirit is the source of the problem. The condition of demon possession does not come about as an accident. The evil spirits have intelligence and are capable of communication. These disembodied spirits are personalities. They seek to inhabit a human personality and, because they are fallen and wicked by nature, seek to emphasize their particular kind of wickedness in the personality they have been able to overcome.

In theological language the cause of the possession is termed "the ground." The ground of possession is that particular sin that has such a hold over the individual that ultimately the evil spirit is able to claim dominion of the personality through the practice of this particular sin. Although there are many grounds of demon possession, the four most dominant are the practice of spiritism, excessive anger, sexual sins and pride.

It is not uncommon for the habitation of an evil spirit in the human personality to produce physical illness. The New Testament mentions demons that caused epilepsy, deafness and dumbness, and, in caused epilepsy, deafness and dumbness, and, in one instance, even the suggestion that fever was caused by an evil spirit.

Demons are capable of causing physical illness. However, physical illnesses directly due to the dominion of an evil spirit over the individual are not the rule but the exception.

It is common for the victim to show dullness with regard to anything spiritual—almost a total failure to comprehend spiritual truth. Quite often there is psychological disturbance. It is important that those who seek to deal with demon possession exercise every care in determining whether or not the individual is actually possessed. Great harm can be done by attempting to deal with a physical and mental condition as though it were demon possession. Such a ministry should be undertaken not by novices, but by experienced and gifted believers. Certainly pastors and elders of the church should give themselves to the study of the biblical teaching with regard to demonism and exorcism.

Divine Healing:
Alliance Life Testimonials

CHAPTER 10

Detour through Suffering

By Adienne Klassen

"You have your miracle. Your digestive organs are functioning properly."

These were the doctor's words to me after I insisted that laboratory tests which had been done twice before be repeated. They marked the end of a four-year journey through a valley of suffering during which I was continuously hospitalized for months on end and often so weak I could only lie in bed.

Stricken at School

When I was thirteen years old I had been called by God to be a missionary to China. Therefore, I enrolled at the Prairie Bible Institute in Three Hills, Alberta, and afterward furthered my preparation for missionary service by taking nurses training at a small hospital in Edmonton.

While waiting for the door of China to open for me, I went back to Prairie for some postgraduate studies, and I supported myself by working part-time in the school's infirmary. That was 1945.

While on duty in the infirmary one afternoon, I noticed that my throat was suddenly very sore. The next morning I had a raging fever and was admitted to the clinic as a patient.

A doctor who was taking classes at the Bible Institute examined me. His diagnosis was, "You have an acute hemolytic streptococcal infection." Subsequently, several other students were stricken, and the source of the infection was traced by the government health service investigators to a cow on a farm from which the school had secured milk.

But none of the other students became as seriously ill as I did, probably because I was physically exhausted. Within hours the infection spread through my body, affecting lungs, stomach, kidneys and spine. Soon I could not move my head nor even my eyes.

Because I could neither move nor speak, the doctors feared that the infection had spread to the base of my brain and destroyed my hearing and optic nerves. But I could hear and see those who were around me. And when he stood over me and looked into my eyes and spoke, I was able to communicate to him, by pressing his hand, that my hearing and sight were functioning.

I remember looking up at him and thinking, "If I could only speak I would tell you that you have lovely blue eyes."

My lungs were soon full of pneumonia, and the infection had affected my spinal cord. I was too sick to be moved to a regular hospital facility. Consequently, I was not expected to live.

However, we who are called according to His purpose are immortal until our work is done. People at the school prayed for me and I survived.

One day during this critical time, there wafted into my room from a radio down the hall, the strains of a gospel song:

> He makes the rose an object of His care,
> He guides the eagle through the pathless air,
> And surely He remembers me.
> My Heavenly Father watches over me.

Through that song God brought comfort and reassurance. I rested in His loving care, and the peace of God flooded my spirit.

Days turned into weeks and weeks into months, and I was still in that infirmary. My temperature remained elevated. Any exertion, even in bed, more than doubled my pulse rate. Eventually when I was able to get out of bed, I found I could not lift my feet.

The principal of the school, Dr. L.E. Maxwell, joined me in prayer for healing. Strangely, at this time, the message that came to both of us was, "My grace is sufficient for thee: for my strength is made perfect in weakness" (2 Corinthians 12:9, KJV). Dr. A.B. Simpson once said, "The pressures of life help us to understand the trials of others and enable us to sympathize with them." God had enrolled me in the school of suffering. Graduation from that training would come in His time. His peace kept vigil over my heart.

At the end of the term at Prairie Bible Institute, I was helpless and hundreds of miles from home. One day while I searched for guidance from the Lord, I opened my Bible and contrary to my normal procedure I began reading where it had opened. Proverbs 27:10 was God's message to me: "Neither go into thy brother's house in the day of thy calamity: for better is a neighbour that is near than a brother far off" (KJV). Instead of trying to go to my home in Saskatoon, I entered the small hospital in Edmonton where I had taken nurses training.

Eventually I returned to Saskatchewan, which I considered to be my home. But my condition did not improve and, if anything, worsened. The fever increased and my heart rate continued to be erratic. Sometimes with my back supported by straps I was able to be in a wheelchair, but most of the time I was in bed. During that three-year period I was hospitalized in Calgary, Edmonton, Saskatoon and Winnipeg. The doctors who were caring for me seemed confused by my symptoms.

Then someone suggested that I contact the Mayo Clinic in Rochester, Minnesota. The local Alliance pastor approached the Red Cross for help. The venture entailed a three-day, 2,400-mile journey by ambulance.

I arrived at Mayo Clinic with a high fever and in a state of collapse, so I was immediately put on round-the-clock penicillin therapy. At once I improved. Before the ten-day course of treatments was finished, my temperature was normal. I was discharged by the clinic to return to Saskatoon and to the care of my family doctor.

But though the infection was apparently gone, my strength did not return. I was still unable to function normally.

At this point I moved to Vancouver to join my father. And almost at once my condition forced me to enter a hospital there.

Fortunately, I was placed under the care of a Christian physician. He ordered tests of my digestive system. When these laboratory reports were analyzed, the doctor shook his head. He said, "I'm sorry. You had that infection too long. Your liver and pancreas have been irreparably damaged. You are in a state of nutritional starvation. This explains your continued weakness. There is nothing more that medicine can do for you."

A few months later summer camp time had come around, and I was taken to a meeting being held on the outskirts of Vancouver. There I heard the testimony of a man who had been wonderfully healed. In obedience to the Word of God, he laid his hands on me and prayed for me. Our joint faith reached up to tap the crimson stream that flows from Calvary. I knew in my heart that I was healed.

To verify this, I went to my doctor and asked that the tests on my digestive system be repeated. And it was then that he pronounced, "Your digestive organs are functioning properly."

Mystery of Suffering

The whys as well as the ways of God are past finding out. I was in His will preparing to go to China, but I was detoured through a valley of suffering. Jesus once made a detour through Samaria to meet the needs of one woman and, through her, a whole city. On my detour I met a young man whom I was able to influence to enter the Christian ministry. Because of that detour I have been able to counsel those who suffer and to encourage many to trust in the Lord for healing.

Although I did not go to China, God has given me

opportunities for ministry. I have served as a deaconness and as a church secretary while doing Sunday school and mission work on the side. From 1974 to 1981 I worked in the office of the Tenth Avenue Alliance Church in Vancouver.

In the twenty-four years following my healing, I missed work only two times because of illness.

CHAPTER

11

From Deathbed to Health: A Surgeon's Story

By Laurel West

For the past sixteen years, Daniel Gordeuk had trusted God to guide his mind and hands as he performed surgeries to help others regain their well-being. Now he lay on an examining table in the x-ray department of the community hospital, hearing a doctor tell him he had prostate cancer that had spread to his bones. A surgeon himself, Dan didn't have to be told his condition was advanced terminal illness. By medical standards, it was hopeless.

But something unusual was happening in that room. There with Dan and the doctor were Dan's wife, Diane, their three-year-old son, David, and Dan's brother, Victor, who is an oncologist. Yet Dan's senses told him they were "in the distance" while another presence filled the room. It was overwhelming and undeniable, and he was certain it was the presence of God. The knowledge of its presence answered a question Dan had harbored for years.

How Real Will God Be?

At the leading of godly parents, Dan had accepted Jesus as his Savior as a child. Throughout his early life and career, he had known God was real, had talked to Him often and depended on Him daily—but Dan had wondered how real God would be to him in the future when he lay dying.

By December 1996, Dan had spent nearly a year suffering from debilitating pain and had endured the misdiagnosis that it was caused by his sciatic nerve. Now, the illness that had secretly stolen his vitality over the last several years had finally come into the open to claim him. But God was there. He was in the room, easing Dan's doubts, enveloping Dan in the certainty that He would not leave him. As if that were not miracle enough, other miraculous things began to happen.

Dan's PSA—the blood test by which doctors diagnose prostate cancer—was 1,300, a count so high that Dan never thought such a reading possible. The cancer had spread throughout his body, excepting only his hands and feet. Doctors at Sloan Kettering Hospital in New York, the foremost cancer treatment facility in the country, confirmed that Dan's condition was terminal. Yet he was determined to ask God for healing.

Because Dan's family had ministered in churches, youth meetings and camps along the Atlantic seaboard, Dan knew and was known by many Christians. "My wife and I are humbled by the thought that as many as 10,000 people might have been praying for me," Dan says. A nurse with whom he had worked some twenty years before wrote the

Gordeuks to say she had heard of Dan's situation, was praying for him and had asked for and received from the Lord a verse just for him. It was Matthew 21:22: "If you believe, you will receive whatever you ask for in prayer." It was a "monumental promise" for Dan, one he held up to the Lord daily. He shared it with everyone he talked to, and word of Dan's faith and his quest for healing spread throughout the community and the region.

A second Gordeuk brother, David, who is a pastor in Kansas, also pleaded with God to give him a verse for Dan. The Lord seemed to lay in his lap Psalm 50:15: "Call upon me in the day of trouble; I will deliver you, and you will honor me." Dan held tightly to that promise, too, and could not have imagined how quickly it would become reality for him.

"And the Lord Shall Raise Him Up"

The day after Dan claimed this verse, a pastor and four other men from his church visited him at home to anoint and pray for him as instructed in James 5:14-15. By that time, Dan was spending most of his day lying on the couch, getting up when the pain was nearly unbearable to go to the tub or shower for relief for his back, ribs and arms, then lying down again. He was anemic, could not bear to sit up for more than five minutes at a time and was taking narcotics around the clock.

As soon as the prayer for healing was finished, Dan pushed against the couch to sit up. Knowing the extent of the pain he had been suffering, the men urged him not to move, but Dan said, "I have to see if I'm healed." To Dan, his rising from the couch that day was literally a "jump" compared with the way he would have done it even minutes before. He saw the men to their cars, and the next day he went deer hunting.

Proof of Healing

The medications were no longer needed because Dan's pain never returned. No medical doctor Dan talked with had ever heard of waxing and waning bone pain in cases of advanced prostate cancer. The doctors at Sloan Kettering advised him to proceed with chemotherapy, which he did. But a mere two weeks after the miraculous disappearance of his pain, before any measurable effect of the treatment could be expected, a nurse called to report on his latest PSA test, and she was beside herself with joy. The count was 61. She said the doctor wanted Dan to have the test done again, in case there was a lab error. When the test was repeated, the count was 27. At the time of this writing, a year and a half after the diagnosis of his cancer, Dan's PSA count is 0.

The only remnant of his illness now, Dan says, is "a wisp of activity in the densest part of the pelvic bones, which is consistent with healing bone, according to the doctors at Sloan Kettering."

A Surgeon for God

Dan is overwhelmed with gratitude for his miracle and for the faith, prayers and God-given assurances expressed by the Christian community from Florida to the Midwest. A great peace has resulted from his experience with cancer. "I'm not afraid of anything anymore," Dan says. "I have this giant of a God standing right beside me. He deemed to heal me, and He trusts me to glorify Him."

How will Dan follow through? He has already given his testimony in churches in New York, Dallas, Oklahoma City, Nashville, Seattle, Toronto and Ottawa, as well as his home church, State College (Pennsylvania) C&MA Church, and others in that state. He has been interviewed on both religious and secular television programs and has participated in a documentary to be aired in the future. Dan and his wife are considering a trip to Africa. There, beginning in Zimbabwe, Dan would volunteer to teach native doctors advanced surgical techniques.

Whenever opportunities arise, Dan will tell his story. By sharing his professional and personal experiences, he believes he can multiply himself as a surgeon for God while glorifying the One who, by His strong and very real hand, brought Dan from death's door to health.

CHAPTER 12

Morgan's Miracle

By Marsha McQueen

On Wednesday, January 27, 1999, I took Morgan Ann, our four-month-old daughter, to the pediatrician. It was supposed to be just a regular check-up with the required shots. However, after examination, the doctor asked me if I had noted any hearing problems. I told her that I had not, but that my husband had mentioned that she never turned her head to find him when he spoke to her from across the room.

In order to conduct a hearing test, the doctor asked me to stand in front of Morgan Ann, who was lying on the examining table, and block her view. She told me that she was going to make a loud noise and that I was not to react so that we could monitor the baby's response. The doctor then closed the door and smacked it hard and loud with a rubber hammer. Morgan Ann did not react. She didn't blink nor flinch nor even turn to find the source of the noise.

With such results, the doctor recommended a more complete hearing examination. I questioned how much we would be able to discern because of her age. She explained that the test would be conducted with sensors on the brain so that no false results could occur. Still convinced that nothing was wrong, I left with the prescription in my hand. *Surely, I would have noticed before now if there was a problem,* I thought to myself.

Back home, Wade and I discussed the situation and came to the realization that something was indeed not right with Morgan Ann's hearing. She had never been comforted by the vacuum or music or any of her musical toys, but only by things that moved or had lights. Now we began to notice that she responded to me only when I was talking directly in front of her, and that a lot of the noises she made were throat noises, not coos. Despair began to set in, and we each in turn began testing her hearing with anything we could think of. Finally, Morgan Ann drifted off to sleep for her afternoon nap.

Wade suggested that we try one test that would either confirm or deny that she had a hearing problem. When she woke up, we would place her in the middle of our bed, with no lights on and nothing around her. Wade would blow his police whistle as loud as he could. Surely, she would jump.

At the appropriate time, he blew the whistle, loud and sudden. I jumped, but alas, the baby did nothing. I was heartbroken and began to question God. How could He have given us such a wonderful blessing as our daughter and then allow her ears to not function? She would never hear my voice sing "Jesus Loves Me" to her, and we might never hear her say sweet words like "Mama," "Daddy" or "I love you." I felt as if my heart would burst from the pain.

After she woke, our older son came into the room carrying one of her musical toys. He crawled up on the bed beside her and said, "Here, Sissy, listen to this!" He pressed the little blue button, and the rocking horse began its tune. No reaction. I ran to the bathroom crying uncontrollably, a thousand thoughts flooding my mind of all the things she would never hear or do or enjoy, problems she would face, hurdles she would have to surmount and the changes that would have to immediately occur in everyone's lives.

Wade came in and hugged me. It was only then, I am ashamed to say, that I was able to turn my fear over to the Lord. I cried for a while, we hugged and I prayed that God would heal her or give us the strength to deal with whatever the diagnosis might be.

The next day, as I went to work, I felt numb, like I was in a cloud, unable to do anything. Wade and I got together for lunch. We shared our hurt and sadness and fears and asked God for grace. As I left him to return to work, I found myself heading to the church. I pulled into the parking lot and waited for the pastor to return from lunch. When he pulled up, I felt the urge to cry, but restrained myself, sure that I had already shed enough tears in the past twenty-four hours to last a lifetime.

He invited me into his office, and I explained what had happened and that Morgan Ann was scheduled for a brain stem auditory response test at Children's Hospital the following Monday (February 1), and that my family desperately needed the church's prayers. We talked for a while about God and faith and surrendering our problems to Him, finding strength in Him. Finally, he reminded me that it is God who can make good out of any circumstances and that it is God who would not forsake us in our time of need if we only turn to Him and ask.

The pastor told me that he would share our concern with some of the elders so that they could pray. Before I left, he prayed for healing for Morgan Ann and for strength and guidance for Wade and me. As I left the church, I felt the first real relief that I had known since this whole experience began.

The next Sunday, before church, I passed the pastor in the hall. He stopped me and said that he would have the elders come forward at the end of the service to pray. Still numb from the possibility that the tiny daughter in my arms would never be able to hear the singing, the lesson or even the laughter of children, I went to help a Sunday school class.

Later, the pastor preached on the healing power of Jesus Christ, and I knew that his message was especially for me and my family. You see, my husband had been saved only a few months. As much as I feared my daughter's potential disability, I also feared that he would turn from God. I watched intently, hoping that he, too, was drawing strength from his faith in God, strength that would get us through this problem.

As the sermon drew to a close, the pastor asked for anyone with a need for healing to come forward. I hugged Morgan Ann close to my chest and told Wade, "Come on, we need to do this for her." My knees were shaking and my body weak. I felt that only by the grace of God would I be able to move to the altar without dropping her or collapsing myself.

We knelt down and began to pray. The pastor came over and asked the elders to lay their hands on us as he anointed Morgan Ann and prayed for us all. I wept openly, laying my heart on the altar and waiting for God to heal her ears. It was more than anything I had ever wanted in my entire life. All the while, I felt that I was surely unworthy of such a miracle.

The next day, the day of the test, finally arrived. We took our son to the baby-sitters and headed to the hospital. My husband carried her in her car seat into the room and placed her on the examination table. The audiologist began typing the information into the computer, and Wade coughed. Morgan Ann startled then went back to sleep.

I began to pray.

"Oh dear Jesus, please Jesus, let us leave here today with a miracle created in our daughter's ears. Please heal her completely as I know only You can. I surrender all to You, Lord! Please help our daughter!"

The audiologist began putting the electrodes on her head and the headphone on her ear, but because she was so small, it wouldn't stay against her ear. As the doctor opened a drawer to get a towel, it squeaked. Morgan Ann jumped again!

The test began, and my praying never stopped. That next thirty minutes seemed like an eternity. I watched the computer screen, desperate to try to make some sense out of the brain waves that were surging across the screen. Finally, the test was done, and the audiologist removed the headphone from her ear. She sat down, looked at us both and said, "This is the part where I am supposed to recommend something to you to help your daughter. However, I cannot."

I felt so confused. How could our baby be beyond help? God would guide us through this, but how, if we could nothing to help her?

The audiologist continued.

"There is nothing wrong with her. All I know is, she is fine now." Our prayers had been answered!

Elated, we left the room. All I could say to our daughter was, "Praise Jesus! You are healed! Praise Jesus, you're fine!" I am sure the people I passed heard me, but that was fine too. In fact, it was better than fine—it was terrific. We all went home, and I felt as if no matter how many times I thanked the Lord, it would never be enough. God had heard little old unworthy me asking for such a big miracle as this, and He smiled, instantly forgiving all of my iniquities, and answered my prayers!

I couldn't wait to call everyone! I started with the pastor. His wife answered, and all I could think to say was, "Deloris, it is Marsha McQueen. Jesus healed her! It's a miracle! She passed! She's fine! There's nothing wrong with her hearing! Praise the Lord!"

A few days later, I was speaking on the phone with the pastor about scheduling Morgan Ann's dedication. He asked me if I would be willing to stand before the congregation the following Sunday and tell everyone what God had done for us. I was nervous, but told him I would be glad to. I knew God would want me to. I prayed repeatedly, intensely, that God would give me the words to say, but time and again, as I rehearsed it in my mind, I came up blank. No words were coming.

Finally, Sunday arrived. I told Wade that I felt he should come forward with me when the time came. I sat nervously through the opening and worried about how I would share this magnificent story. Once more, I turned it over to God and asked Him to give me the words to say. However, when the pastor called us forward, Wade began to speak. He told the congregation that after I had talked to the pastor about our problem and we turned it over to God, that he noticed a difference in little Morgan Ann. He said that that same day, he saw her respond when he coughed. He said that when our friend Jerry held her in church that Sunday before the test and the Sunday school bell rang, she responded. And he said that, most importantly, of all, when the elders laid their hands on us in prayer he felt "just a feeling" come over him. He didn't know what it was, and he didn't question it. He just knew at that point that everything was going to be OK.

We now watch our daughter coo at us and imitate our sounds. She looks for us when we talk and jumps when a noise startles her. We thank God for our blessings and the miracle He performed in our lives that day.

Pastor MacElwee told me that all things happen for a reason, that they are all in God's plan. Often times we cannot see what that plan is until it has passed, and we look back on it. I have rarely stopped reflecting on the experience and now understand what he meant.

I know why this happened in my life, my family, my church. You see, I had always felt so unworthy of God's grace and power, and He used this to show me that even though I am a sinner He will still love me and keep me as long as I believe in Him and His saving grace.

My husband, too, experienced the awesome power of the Lord Jesus Christ. Our faith has been strengthened. Praise the Lord! And finally, our church was blessed with the opportunity to see what was truly a work of God.

If you cross someone's path who has begun to doubt that God still performs miracles, please tell them how He performed a miracle in our lives through our daughter, Morgan Ann.

CHAPTER 13

I Am a Living Miracle

By Nelson Price

That November morning of 1976 in Flushing, Michigan, was crisp. I scraped the frost off the pickup windshield as I headed for the school where I taught.

Out on the highway the windshield began to fog. *Better stop and wipe it off,* I reasoned. No use taking chances.

I was doing about forty-five when I eased over onto the shoulder—and connected squarely with an unyielding lowbed trailer getting ready to take on some earth-moving machinery.

Somehow I was aware that I was lying across the seat of my truck and that it was hard for me to breathe. The next thing I remember, someone was pounding on the door where my head was and a policeman was over my body trying from inside to get that door open—"so we can get you out," he explained.

"Why don't you take me out the same door you got in?" I asked. I remember him grabbing me by my ankles and dragging me across the seat. Although I was aware of what was happening, that was the last sensation of feeling I had until my wife took my hand later in the emergency room of the hospital in Flint.

I was alert enough to ask them to call my school and let them know I would not be there that day. I also asked them not to use the siren on the ambulance because it bothered my head.

Once in the Flint hospital, I drifted in and out of consciousness. I knew they were trying to syringe fluid out of the heart sac, but I felt absolutely nothing. The absence of pain was a miracle in itself. I would have been more concerned had I realized that their references to my "purple" neck and face and ears meant I had turned blue. When you turn blue you don't have enough oxygen; you're not getting blood where you need it.

I was conscious long enough to ask the doctors if I might pray before they began surgery. It was a rather perfunctory prayer. I simply said, "Lord, just take care of things," and that was exactly the way I felt. They would check me out and I'd go home that night and be ready for school the next day. Or so I thought.

It wasn't quite that way. Down in the waiting room where my wife and our pastor, Rev. Neil H. McDowell, and some Christian friends were standing vigil, a nurse came in to announce that they were losing me. Pastor McDowell said, "We need to pray harder," so they joined hands and prayed again.

What they didn't know was that I was already clinically dead. When the doctors opened up my abdominal cavity, they found my liver in shambles and the arteries all torn up. The heart sac was full of blood. The major and minor venae cavae had been ripped loose; one of the valves had been damaged.

For twelve minutes my heart did not beat. After three minutes without a heartbeat doctors anticipate brain damage. At the end of seven minutes the surgeons can quit—the patient is legally dead. Twelve minutes after my heart stopped after the fifth electric shock, it started beating again and the surgeons saw the possibility of getting me off the operating table—so I could die somewhere else.

They crisscrossed my liver with surgical tape to hold it together and then closed the incision as quickly as they could, sending me out to intensive care where they were sure I would never regain consciousness.

About 4 o'clock that afternoon I woke up and saw my wife standing beside the bed. She looked like a total disaster—I don't know any other way to describe it—and I was so full of tubes and so tied down that I couldn't say a thing or make a move. So I gave her a big wink—that's all I could do!

It was enough. She realized that I couldn't be too bad off if I could wink. The concern and the fear just seemed to fall from her, neater than anything.

When she came in at 6 o'clock (in intensive care you are granted a five-minute visit every hour) I motioned as though I had a pencil in my hand and wanted to write. When my wife asked the nurses for pencil and paper they thought she had taken leave of her senses.

Carefully I wrote, "Water on my lips." I was thirsty and I figured a little water on my lips might help.

When she came in at 7 o'clock I asked for paper and pencil again and wrote, "He's doing a miracle." It was the reassurance my wife and family needed from God.

So it went. Finally the doctors and the hospital realized that maybe I was going to survive after all. This posed a problem for them. The tape used to hold my liver together had to come out, and the doctors weren't quite sure it could be done without everything coming apart.

The surgeon who had taped me up had had some experience in Vietnam. He frankly told us his success ratio: He had lost every patient he had worked on with this kind of damage. And he wasn't anxious to lose another.

They called Ann Arbor, but no one down there held out any hope. Finally we decided that the man who put the tape on was the man who should take it off.

People literally from coast to coast were praying as the time of surgery approached. Never before did I so appreciate the full meaning of the phrase "the family of God."

All the blood in the hospital was in the operating room and the other two hospitals in Flint were on standby should more be needed.

I was aware of the seriousness of the operation. It's a feeling beyond description when you know that if anything happens—if you don't come off that operating table alive—you're going to walk into the presence of God!

Again before surgery I prayed—this time with much more feeling than before. And God worked another miracle.

But once back in the regular ward, I became impatient. I've never been one to want to sit around very long; I like to go and to do and to be independent.

One day our pastor's wife, knowing my impatience, came in and began to lecture me on the subject. Suddenly she was in tears and I realized she was really concerned about me. So I thought maybe I had better be concerned, too.

"Myrtle," I promised, "I'll be patient and only do what the doctors and nurses say I can. And I won't only promise you, but I'll promise God at the same time."

It was not until a few days later that I began to know the implications of that promise. My heart started to enlarge. The hospital's head cardiologist came in and opened up the records. Each time he turned a page he shook his head.

"Mr. Price, any one of the four things that were wrong with you was enough to kill you," he said.

"I have a heavenly Father who loves me a lot," I responded.

All the heart tests proved negative. So they did a heart catheterization, and beyond the heart itself they found a bulge on the aorta. A bit of excitement, and pop! All would be over for me.

I could have figured that I'd been through enough. But God was faithful to the promise about patience I had made, and I didn't get upset.

"This time," the doctor said, "you go to Houston."

He told me about Dr. Dan Cooley—"the fastest knife in the West"—who does twelve to twenty open-heart surgeries in a day and has to know what he is doing.

I was not particularly excited about going to Houston, but I told the Lord that if there were people there who needed to be talked to, I was willing to take my witness down there.

The surgery was scheduled for December 13—a Monday morning. In the operating room I was just taking a breath to ask them if we could pray before they started when I went out. I woke up in intensive care, the surgery successfully behind me, God once more vindicating a promise He had earlier given my wife and me: "This poor man cried, and the LORD heard him; he saved him out of *all* his troubles (Psalm 34:6, italics mine).

On January 29, 1977, I went back to full-time schoolteaching. In February I played eighteen minutes of church-league basketball. That's a miracle!

Lives have been changed as the result of what I have been through, and they are still being changed. God has not only worked a miracle in my body, He has worked miracles in men's souls. When I think that God has chosen me to be part of something like that it makes me shouting happy.

Every morning when I kick my feet over the edge of the bed and find that I can get up by myself I say, "God, thank You for this day. I'm going to enjoy it, every minute of it, because You have given *me* this day."

I'm on borrowed time. God has given me each day, and each is special.

Last March, a year and four months after the accident, I had another checkup. All the tests were reassuring. My heart is better than it has ever been. I am under absolutely no physical restrictions.

It's exciting when we see an answer to prayer. But if you think *that* is exciting, try *being* the answer to prayer and find out how exciting that is!

Then you will know how I feel!

CHAPTER 14

A Walking Miracle

By Dorothy F. Barefoot

I made up my mind that I would be content and not ask again for healing. Then suddenly I became a walking miracle.

I went to the YWCA where eighteen girls of different faiths had seen me week in and week out with a leg that was twisted and turned and wasted. I stood before them in God's power, slipped into the water and said, "Praise the Lord!"

I went to my doctor. He knew that it was something beyond medical means. "You are a walking miracle," he said, happy and excited to see that God had done something that medicine could not.

I thank God for giving me, back in 1972, the promise in Isaiah that "They that wait upon the LORD shall renew their strength; they shall mount up with wings as eagles; they shall run, and not be weary; and they shall walk, and not faint" (Isaiah 40:31, KJV).

I needed that promise in 1972. It was early December, and I was driving with a friend and her daughter on the way to do some shopping when a truck pulled out in front of us at an intersection.

In the crash that followed, two of us were hurt very seriously.

My husband and son arrived before the ambulance, and before they followed me to the hospital they had alerted the C&MA Church in York, Pennsylvania. My pastor, Rev. David K. Muir, immediately activated the church prayer chain, then rushed to the hospital to be there with prayer and with his presence.

As I slipped in and out of consciousness I knew that I was having difficulty breathing. I felt so bad that I turned my face to the wall.

"Lord," I prayed, "I am ready to go. There is only one thing I ask: Don't let my family become bitter. Put Your hand upon them and keep them safe."

For several weeks my life hung in the balance. Although I did not realize it, there had been brain damage. I tried to concentrate on God's Word, but the verses were mixed and muddled. One night it was as though God's Word appeared to me in a special revelation:

> They that wait upon the LORD shall renew their strength; they shall mount up with wings as eagles; they shall run, and not be weary; and they shall walk, and not faint. (Isaiah 40:31, KJV)

At the time I was not able to walk. They had operated twice on my leg and there was no feeling in it at all. They told me that I had muscle damage and that I would have to use a walker and wear heavy shoes to pull the muscles back to where they belonged. I would also need a leg brace.

After my discharge from the hospital I returned three days a week for therapy. Gradually, after many weeks, I learned to get around with the walker. I began water therapy at the YWCA pool. Still there was no coordination in my leg.

Although far from well, I persuaded my husband that August to let me go to nearby Summit Grove Camp for the summer Bible conference. Our daughter, in training to be an x-ray technician, had time off before beginning her second year; she and two others would care for me at camp.

Fortified by that happy prospect, I spent long hours struggling to learn to walk with crutches. My husband worked with me three solid hours each evening. "Left, right, left, right, . . ." My daughter and others helped, too.

But it was a slow process. My balance was off. If I took my eyes from the ground and my feet, I would forget what to do and fall.

From one day to the next I noticed that I could do something that I had not been able to do before.

I thought of Paul who had asked God three times for healing. Paul said that we should be content in whatsoever state we are. I made up my mind that I would be content and not ask again for healing. The Lord already had given me so much. I looked back and saw all His blessings and committed the situation to Him.

Although I continued to improve, the anniversary of the accident came around, and I had not recovered. I had mentally set that date as the point when I could again drive the car and return to my nursing job. On my next visit to the therapist he told me there was nothing more that he could do for my leg. I was very discouraged.

"Dorothy," the doctor said at my next appointment, as I shared my frustration, "look back to a year ago, and to six months ago. You are getting better, but it is slow. We can't put a time limit on this. And besides"—he looked at the crutch—"what is wrong with going through life with a crutch?"

By March I still was not well. The insurance coverage had expired and we had a therapy bill of more than a thousand dollars. My blood count was low and the doctor said I needed rest.

That weekend my brother took me to see my father. On the way home, as my brother was complaining about all the family problems, I said to him, "You know, God is so good!"

"What did God ever do for you?" he shot back.

"He saved me!" I replied.

I was burdened for this brother of mine. Our church was showing a film, "A Thief in the Night," during the Sunday school hour the following Sunday. I invited my brother and his wife to see it. I also invited a therapist's aid whose personal tragedies had given us something in common and to whom I had witnessed.

The film was followed by a Sunday morning evangelistic service. My brother and his family were there. So was my friend, the therapist's aid. At the invitation, my sister-in-law went forward, tears streaming down her face.

Should I go up and pray with her? Or stay with the friend I had invited? I went forward, laid down my crutch, and knelt, my arms around my sister-in-law.

After she had gotten through to God, we talked together. She was disappointed that my brother, her husband, had not gone forward.

"Marie," I said, "God has called *you* and you must take your stand. Nothing is impossible with God."

As I said it, God's power came down. With our arms around each other we felt His presence. Suddenly I found myself *walking* at the front of the church with perfect balance, praising God. I walked back to my seat and sat down beside my friend who was still waiting.

"My leg feels so tight," I exclaimed. My friend looked down at it.

"Look at it, Dorothy!" she said. The leg, wasted from sixteen months of disuse, was filling out. My husband reached down and removed the brace and my leg became perfectly straight. And it filled out just like the other one. I know that if I had needed three toes that Sunday morning, God would have put them on!

Pastor Muir called on me for a testimony. All I could say was that God had done the impossible. He had touched me and made me completely whole. My mind, unable to retain new information since the accident, also cleared up.

I think of how God worked things out when the therapist was frustrated, the doctor gave me no hope, my family was resigned to an invalided wife and mother and insurance had run out. At that point God acted. He has worked out every detail, even to the payment of all my medical bills.

God deserves all the praise. He is the only One who could have done what He has done.

Divine Healing:
The Power, the Pain and the Promise

CHAPTER

15

God Is Real: The Story of Jacques Béchard

By Jesse Jespersen

No genuine Christian would deny that the God of the Bible is a God who is real (that He exists). Such a belief is foundational to our faith and our approach to Him. "Anyone who comes to [God] must believe that he exists [that He is real]" (Hebrews 11:6). The balance of this verse challenges us to also believe that He is alive, "that he is in a state of action," the dictionary definition for alive. "And that he rewards those who earnestly seek him," that we can and should expect Him to speak, give direction and guidance to our lives and experience His power and presence. This is where many who believe God is real part company with those who also believe that He is alive.

It is our sincere desire and prayer that the following testimony and commentary will serve to help us all come to a stronger conviction that God indeed is real and alive. May it enable many to experience His presence, guidance and spiritual and physical healing when needed, to learn what it means to experience God as one "[walks] through the valley of the shadow of death" (Psalm 23:4), to better understand what He means when He says, "My thoughts are not your thoughts, neither are your ways my ways" (Isaiah 55:8), to know "I am the LORD that healeth [you]" (Exodus 15:26, KJV) even when He does not do so instantly but chooses a longer, even painful process, so He can reveal that He is indeed real and alive.

In March 1996, in Lévis, Québec, Jacques Béchard, a medical doctor himself, made the frightening discovery that he had a nine centimeter cancerous growth at the level of the lumbar spine. If he wanted to have a chance of getting better, he would need to have chemotherapy. Here is his testimony.

"In October 1994, by God's grace, I discovered a large ganglion in the groin area which, after biopsy, proved to be a lymphoma. It was believed that there was no other growth, and everything else was normal. An error was made in reading the CAT scan at that time and it was only a year and a half later that it was discovered. In 1994, after radiation therapy, I considered myself healed and believed God had allowed me to discover this cancer in time. It was during this time that I began to read my Bible and pray, and I accepted Jesus Christ as my personal Savior. My wife had already been a believer for nineteen years.

"So here I was, a year and a half later in March of 1996 with cancer and the advice of my doctor to have chemotherapy. It was at this moment that I decided to place everything in God's hands because after twenty years of a family medical practice, the very discipline I had so often defended had let me down for over a year and a half and now could only offer me doubts and worry. I knew what chemotherapy could do, and in spite of and because of that knowledge, I was afraid.

"So it was I decided to put everything into God's hands and that from then on, only He would be my Guide. I first asked Him to clearly show me, yes or no, if I was to take chemotherapy and that the answer would come from His Word at the place of my daily reading. Up to this point in my Christian experience, I had never asked God in this way and had no experience in receiving answers from Him.

"Is God real and alive? Can we expect Him to act, to speak? I took my Bible with a confidence that came only from God and quickly found myself at the passage where Jesus was praying in the Garden of Gethsemane. It became very clear that I, too, was to say to Jesus, 'Father, . . . take this cup from me. Yet not what I will, but what you will' (Mark 14:36).

"There was no more doubt in my mind and heart, I was to go through chemotherapy. I didn't understand why, nor did I try to understand. I simply knew I was to do it and I would do so because it was what God wanted. I went for my first treatment with the firm conviction that I already had my healing from cancer and that it was only a matter of time until that would be confirmed by the doctor.

"I still clearly remember the words of the hematologist who came to see me before I would have my first treatment, while the nurse was starting my first intravenous solution. 'Not only will your hair fall out, but your beard as well.' Three weeks later, before the second treatment, the thought came to me to ask the Lord to keep me from losing my hair. However, thinking it was a question of pride because of my appearance, I said to myself that I couldn't make such a request. The next morning when I awoke, it was as if a voice was saying to me to ask the Lord that I not lose my hair, and this time I had the conviction that I was to do so. So I did, and that same day my daily reading brought me to Luke 12:6-7: 'Are not five sparrows sold for two pennies? Yet not one of them is forgotten by God. Indeed, the very hairs of your head are all numbered. Don't be afraid; for you are worth more than many sparrows.' It's hard to describe what I felt when I read that all the hairs of my head were counted. Upon receiving such a clear answer after having just made my request, the presence of God became palpable in me. I knew He was with me. He was my support, my comfort. Shortly after this, without my asking, God gave me this additional assurance from Luke 21:18: 'But not a hair of your head will perish.' "

As God promised, Jacques did not lose any of his hair even though he eventually received all the chemotherapy treatments. Can we expect God to speak? Can we expect Him to manifest His presence and power? The answer is, beyond any shadow of doubt, a resounding YES.

"I continued to ask the Lord if I had to follow through with my treatments, sure that at any moment He would tell me to stop. After three more treatments over a period of three months, the hematologist decided I should have another CAT scan on June 6, 1996. I was sure it would confirm that I was healed. I remember as if it were yesterday the words of my radiologist who examined the films. 'There is no real progression of the cancerous mass, but there is also no regression.' I couldn't believe my ears!

" 'That's impossible,' I told him, so sure was I that I was healed. My wife had to insist I leave the hospital. I returned home totally devastated, and I could only find refuge in the arms of my God.

"A few days later my hematologist suggested another type of treatment with which I had less than forty-seven percent chance of a remission. I didn't know what to think, but since the Bible says to be submissive to those over us, I accepted his advice. The first treatment of this new series would begin July 27. I felt very insignificant when I went for the first treatment which would take place over three days every four weeks. I was to receive three different medications. I met the hematologist who gave the prescription to the nurse and I began to have my first treatment in the chemotherapy room. The hematologist came to see me during this treatment. I was reading my Bible. In reply to his question of what I was reading, he took my Bible and turned the pages until he found Romans 8:28: 'We know that all things work together for good to them who love God.' I asked him what he intended in reading me this verse. His reply was that it was the only verse he knew in the Bible, and I could do with it what I wanted. I thanked him, saying it was a wonderful promise, to which he simply replied, 'So much the better.' I remained perplexed at this seemingly divine intervention through an individual who didn't seem to even know God or give much importance to Him, and yet who gave me this promise from His Word. Little did I realize at the time the full impact this intervention would have in my life. Does God truly intervene in our lives?

"I received my three days of treatment as planned. Four weeks later I returned for the second series of treatments, and the hematologist on duty ordered a blood test to see if the level of my white blood cells was acceptable. I was feeling extremely weak and wasn't surprised to learn that I had practically no white cells and severe anemia. I was advised to return in a week. I again asked the Lord if I should continue my treatments, and He showed me practically every time through His Word that I should submit to what was ordered. A week later nothing had changed, and I was once again sent home after an injection of a marrow stimulant. I returned home very troubled and I once again asked God for guidance. On one hand the Bible was telling me to submit to my treatment; on the other, the doctors were refusing to give it to me. I asked God to enlighten me and as always, it came from my Bible reading that very day from Acts 27:33-34 and in a very spectacular way: 'Just before dawn Paul urged them all to eat. "For the last fourteen days," he said, "you have been in constant suspense and have gone without food—you haven't eaten anything. Now I urge you to take some food. You need it to survive. Not one of you will lose a single hair from his head." ' First of all, I was once again impressed by the reference to not losing a hair, and I knew God was once again speaking to me. I reread the passage to better understand what God was saying to me. Effectively, I was fourteen days behind in my treatments, but I was to receive them. I went to the hospital and my white cells had greatly increased, so I was able to have the treatment.

"To my consternation they discovered that when I received the first treatment, an error was made and I had received a triple dose on July 27-29. The medication that I had received in triple dose was a 'blue' medication, easily identifiable. Normally the protocol says that I should have received it the first day, but not on days two or three. I had had it all three days. The hematologist had made a mistake, and he had mentioned beforehand that this drug could be 'hard' on the heart. When I realized this error which was confirmed by my hematologist that day, I sensed a great anger boiling up in me, but it only lasted a few minutes. I realized that the one responsible for the error was the man who had searched my Bible and read me Romans 8:28. I realized not only did God ask me to receive the treatments, but He also was deciding what I should receive, and this was always confirmed by His Word. My anger disappeared and I was convinced that this triple dose was necessary for my healing even though I was extremely weak. I felt my strength decreasing with each day. Even though I had only two series of treatments, my hematologist asked that I have another CAT scan at the end of September.

"Since I felt so weak, I asked the Lord if I should have another treatment. I had just read the story of Gideon, so I asked for a different sign than something from His Word. This was a Thursday in September, 1996. I went to bed without an answer. Friday morning I received a telephone call from a pastor I knew somewhat from having met him on several occasions. He asked if I'd be home that afternoon as he wished to pay me a visit. That afternoon he and his wife came and said God had told him to give me this seven-word message (in French): 'In the Name of Jesus Christ, be healed.' "

Here we need to back up to Tuesday of that same week. I, Jesse Jespersen, the pastor in question, was spending the morning in prayer when as clearly as if I'd heard an audible voice in my office, I heard, "Go and say to Jacques Béchard, 'Jacques, in the Name of the Lord Jesus, be healed.' " This set off a time of discussion with God which I recorded in my journal. "I hardly know Jacques; he's not even in my church. What about the sixteen-year-old girl with Hodgkin's Disease in our church? My faith is too small to do this."

To all my questions and arguments, the answer was always the same: "None of that is your concern; just do what I ask." Finally, with both fear and an unusual sense of God's presence I wrote, "All right, Lord, I'll go." I went home that afternoon and shared with my wife what had happened.

Her reply was, "If God told you to do it, you better obey." This was Tuesday. Wednesday we could not go. Jacques lives in Ste-Claire, thirty-five kilometers (twenty-one miles) outside of our city. Thursday we were going through there to visit some folks in another town and thought we could combine the two visits. In the end, that became impossible. Finally, Friday I called and that afternoon, delivered the message God had given. (Remember that it was Thursday that Jacques had asked for a sign or word from God.) Now back to Jacques' testimony . . .

"When I heard those seven words, it took me several minutes to realize that this visit was the sign of healing I'd asked God for. In spite of my extreme weakness, I felt the greatness of my God who spoke to me, dust among the dust. I need to state that at this moment and for the following months, my relationship with God developed in an extraordinary manner.

"Two weeks later I was to have another CAT scan, and while praying, I sensed that things were happening very quickly in my life. I took my Bible and the Lord showed me the exact moment of my healing. In my daily reading, I was gripped by Second Corinthians 6:2: 'In the time of my favor I heard you, and in the day of salvation I helped you. I tell you, now is the time of God's favor, now is the day of salvation.'

"This verse, probably one of the most precious for me in all the Bible, hit me like a brick. The Lord was telling me that my healing was confirmed and now I was to tell someone. I was to give testimony to that effect. So the next day I went to our little church group in St. Isidor, and with God's blessing, gave testimony that I was completely healed. The little group present was flabbergasted. I had no medical proof of my healing, but I had to say it. I had to testify that I was healed. I couldn't resist, I had to give testimony to my healing.

"That very evening I continued in my Bible reading. My praying was directed to asking for a second sign, which I did, since He had indicated to me the exact time of my healing from the Bible. I had the impression that my wife and I were the only ones who understood what I was experiencing spiritually. I was being carried along by such a forceful enthusiasm, in spite of only having three quarts of blood in my body. That evening I, like Gideon, courageously asked for a second sign, a tangible proof for me and for those to whom I testified, for all who smiled at me when I did, who shared my enthusiasm and were sympathetic, and for all those who still had a look of unbelief.

"The next day I arose as usual and about an hour later, my wife opened the mail and received the results of the CAT scan I had had about ten days earlier. There was an important regression in the ganglion. The nine to ten centimeter mass had begun to disappear.

"It was probably this Monday morning at the end of September 1996 when all that the Lord had showed me from His Word was medically confirmed and that I realized the power and love of my God. He had been and continued to look after me, an infinitely small part of His creation. I am important to Him as are all humans on the earth, but it is not a question of merit. I simply had asked Him to give me faith to pray. He gave me this faith, and that Monday He increased my faith. I also realized that He had directed my prayer. He told me what I ought to ask, what He was prepared to give me, and I only had to listen to what the Holy Spirit was saying to me. Thus I understood that it was He who had told me to ask Him to keep my hair from falling out at the beginning of my treatments. This was an outward sign that He was taking care of me and even though the first CAT scans were not encouraging about what was happening on the inside of me, He was showing me by conserving my hair and beard that He was taking care of all the details.

"I had a great need to understand these truths so that I would continue to take my treatments as He once again showed me from His Word. I wanted to stop them as everybody, including the hematologists, were optimistic about my case. They, however, suggested that I have another four series of treatments.

"Two months later, at the end of November, my hematologist ordered a new CAT scan. I was very sure what the results would be, and I no longer saw things as before. I remember well wishing that I had been up to Second Corinthians 6:2 in my reading, but unfortunately I was not, as I mentioned to my wife. However, the morning of December 1, just before going for my scan, I turned the page on the calendar on my desk near the kitchen table to find, written in bold letters, that the verse of the month was, 'Now is the time of God's favor, now is the day of salvation.' I understood immediately that God was speaking to me, and that it was by this verse, forever engraved on my mind, that God was sealing His promise of healing. God never abandons us. He knew my weakness and my needs, and He reminded me again of His care from the Word.

"I therefore had my CAT scan in December 1996, notwithstanding an extreme weakness, a severe neuropenury (lack of white blood cells, our internal defense mechanism against germs), an anemia of eight grams of hemoglobin (half the normal) and an infectious colitis caused by a germ called 'clostridium,' which was causing me to have ten to twenty bowel movements a day (a secondary effect of my treatments). In spite of my doctor's fears about my precarious state of health, which could very quickly have degenerated toward death at any moment, I learned early in December of 1996 that the retroperitoneal mass had virtually disappeared. Medically I was on the way to remission; spiritually I knew I was healed of cancer, but I felt so very weak that for an instant I felt I might die from the secondary effects of the treatments.

"On December 4, because of my deteriorating state of health, and in spite of the good x-ray results, I asked the Lord for enlightenment. That same day He answered me from His Word in Mark 16:18: 'They will pick up snakes with their hands; and when they drink deadly poison, it will not hurt them at all.' I then understood that, in spite of my extreme weakness, the secondary effects of my treatments would not sweep me away because God's Word had said the opposite. I also realized again how small and frail I was, so easily shaken when I looked elsewhere than to my Lord.

"In February of 1997, for the first time since the beginning of my treatments, my doctor spoke to me of 'healing' and not of 'remission,' although when I had started my treatments it was with only a forty-seven percent chance of remission.

"Like my hair which I should have lost and never did, I know that the Lord controls all, and that my healing came from Him. He directed my treatments, and I know that probably it had to be that way for hundreds of reasons which I can't understand, but that maybe someday I will understand. But I know that the Lord is always faithful to His Word.

"Since that time, my life has completely changed. Today, in 2000, I am healed and in good physical shape. I have once again taken up my work as a family physician, but with a totally different perspective. I know that God is with me, that He is near me and that He is alive. In the past I always tried to give the maximum of myself to my patients with all the sincerity of which I was capable, but I often did it to my own physical and psychological detriment and I didn't rely on God. Today I do my work with the same sincerity, the same devotion, but I do it with my God, in His presence. I pray for my patients, and even sometimes, with some of them in my office, and I put them into God's hands. What a comfort, what support, what consolation to be able to put these suffering folks into the hand of a God who is all powerful and who loves them all!

"I often have the feeling that I am in waiting for something that I am going to do later for the Lord. I listen to what He says to me and I go to Him in all my difficulties. I know that He wanted what He did in my life so I can help others who have serious illnesses. I also know that Jesus, who while on earth healed the sick, wants to do the same today for those who want it and who believe in Him. I know that we must trust Him completely, and I know that it is He who gives us the strength to trust Him.

"I've had several occasions to give my testimony, and I know that the Lord will ask me to serve Him, in His time and His way. I have no worries about that because I know, that here as well, it is He who gives the strength and wisdom to do it, and I simply want to be in His plan for what He wants of me."

In the later part of 1996, Jacques and his family began attending the Alliance church in Lévis, Québec. Jacques' journey through the valley of the shadow of death in which he learned that God is real and alive had an impact in our congregation in strengthening that same conviction in our hearts. Not only do we believe that He will speak, give direction and guidance, manifest His power and presence, but we also expect Him to do so. And He does, which makes living for Him an exciting experience.

CHAPTER

16

Knife at Her Throat

By Sanford Hashimoto

Brazil is a fascinating country of vast lands, the size of the continental USA. It is also a country with multiple nationalities and cultures. My wife, Wendie and I came to Brazil as missionaries in 1980. We were greeted by missionaries who helped us get settled into the culture, language, house, etc. We did not know a single word of Portuguese. We needed to buy food for the family but did not know where to go, nor how to say "bread, milk, eggs and meat." Neither did we know how to use the currency. We were totally lost! We saw strange things—the police with huge automatic weapons in the streets and near government buildings, animal sacrifices and spirit center signs above store fronts.

Walking around downtown Porto Alegre, you will see many modern buildings, shops, restaurants and beautiful parks, but as you zig-zag your way through the hundreds of neighborhoods and carefully observe the surroundings, you may see some unusual objects. On the street intersection, for instance, there may be a red crepe paper plate with popcorn, candles, a clay bowl and very often, a dead chicken. These are symbols of *umbanda* (African voodooism). The amazing thing is that the *gauchos* (cowboys), the nickname given to all those from this region, are not mainly black Africans, but white Italians, Poles and Germans. When we first arrived, we were amazed to see so many blond and blue-eyed people!

The power of Satan is so strong. Demons possess these spiritist followers. I remember Marcelo, a beautiful ten-year-old boy with blue eyes and blond hair. He was the terror of the block. He hit the little ones, broke neighbors' flowers and plants and scribbled graffitti on walls. The teachers could not stand him; he was moved from school to school. We came to know him when his mother, Clarisa, asked for our help. At the time, she had a black eye, scratches on her face and was in despair. Marcelo had beaten her up. Clarisa believed her son had demons.

They were living in a rented storage room in the back of a house. We prayed and fasted before going to visit them and were able to destroy the articles Clarisa was using in her spirit worship. As we talked to her, her son came in and with an authoritarian voice demanded to know who we were and why we were there. He then commanded us to leave his house and never to return.

Wendie, myself and Rosa, another woman from our church, tried to speak to him in love, but he was very abusive in both words and actions. Before our very eyes, he even tried to strangle the cat that happened to walk into the room.

Then, suddenly, he grabbed two knives and began to slash at me. Thankfully, he could not touch us for we claimed protection by the blood of Jesus Christ our Savior. We prayed out loud for the demons to leave, and we quoted Scripture verses and sang gospel songs. Marcelo jumped on top of his mother's sewing machine, challenged us and then jumped alongside his mother, placing the knives at her throat. He screamed that he would cut her head off . . . but just then, Wendie, with the courage and authority of the Lord Almighty, gently took the knives out of his hands.

We grabbed the ten-year-old and were able to pin him to the floor despite the fact that he had the strength of an adult. We prayed and quoted Scriptures. For what seemed like hours, but were only minutes, we continued to pray and sing.

Marcelo calmed down and apparently did not know what had happened to him. He was like a new person and asked for water to drink. As he was drinking, he spat the water in the face of Rosa and ran away laughing. We waited for him to return, but he never did. We told his Clarisa to bring him to our Wednesday night prayer meeting so we as a church could pray for them and trust God for complete victory.

To our surprise, they showed up. They were gladly welcomed, and they listened to our singing and the Bible study. During the meeting, Clarisa shared how God had done a miracle in the life of Marcelo. Though he had run away, he came back a new person! He no longer screamed, nor hit others. He even told his mother how much he loved her.

To our amazement, then, he began to quote the Scripture passages I had just read to the congregation and sang some of the words to the songs we were singing. Though he did not know how to read because he could not be taught in schools, he demonstrated great intelligence.

As the days and months passed, Marcelo learned to read and write. He was in school and became a top student. The neighborhood children now played with him, and he brought the neighbors to church. The Lord Jesus Christ completely changed his life and showed His power to overcome Satan and his demons.

Jesus Christ is Lord! Jesus Christ is the same yesterday, today and forever!

CHAPTER 17

God Healed Me of Hodgkin's Disease

By Timothy Owen

In the fall of 1958, my senior year at Wilson High School in Portland, Oregon, I noticed that the lymph nodes in my neck were swollen. My parents and others noticed, too, as the swelling increased. I went to our family doctor, a general practitioner, for a diagnosis. He thought it was just the result of an infection that would soon pass. My sister provided baby-sitting for a family, the father/husband of which was an internist. One evening when he came to pick up my sister to do some baby-sitting, he gave me a cursory exam. He was concerned, and so he requested that I come in for an appointment with him in his office the next day.

A biopsy was performed soon thereafter. The results were positive. I had Hodgkin's Disease. The doctor ordered a schedule of radiation treatments. As I began to undergo those treatments, I was warned not to allow any trauma to the radiated areas. Before being diagnosed with this cancer, I was on the wrestling team which I, of course, had to quit. However, perhaps because I was in denial and certainly being careless, one day after school, as I was watching the wrestling team, I gave in to the temptation to wrestle a little bit.

Soon the cancer metastasized, spreading throughout my body. I had swollen lymph glands in every location where they existed, including elbows, armpits, knees and, most critically, my chest. I also began to experience other symptoms such as night sweats, severe weight loss and increasing pain. Gradually I reached the point where I was critically ill.

My parents, being long-time members of the church with good teaching on divine healing, called for the elders of the church to anoint me and pray for me. They also called in other pastors and evangelists to pray for me. My sense of the spiritual significance of this event was small. As far as I was concerned, I was just sick and bewildered about it. I don't remember praying much about it or struggling with God or even having a fear of death. I did take comfort in my belief that I wasn't the only one who had gone through this kind of thing. Others had been able to handle it; I could too.

I have often wondered if perhaps God was using this more in my mother's spiritual life at the time than in mine. I do remember her being in great turmoil and in much prayer about this situation. I really see her as the main player, spiritually, in this whole scene with me having a supporting role.

At that point I was admitted to the hospital. The doctors had to use very strong medication to alleviate my pain and allow me to sleep. Every morning I would awaken, step on the scales and find myself another five pounds lighter. The doctor prescribed a dose of primitive chemotherapy called Nitrogen

Mustard. One dose was administered. My condition worsened.

I hated being in the hospital and convinced my mother to persuade the doctor to let me go home. My mother told me later that she and the doctor had a conversation about my prognosis. It was Wednesday, and he predicted that by the weekend I would be in a coma, at which time an ambulance would transport me back to the hospital where the medical people would care for me until I died.

But mother had heard from God. He wanted to heal me. "Doctor," she said, "God is going to heal my son."

The doctor, being a wonderful man, but an agnostic, paternalistically responded, "That's fine. You hang on to that faith. You're going to need it."

Mom said, "No, God's going to heal him."

I was overjoyed to be back in the comforts of home and out of the sterile, lonely hospital with its tasteless food. I immediately began to heal. I ate lots of mom's great meals and began to gain weight. The symptoms of night sweats and pain left. That Sunday I went to church and the next day, Monday, I returned to school. My classmates and teachers were delightfully surprised to see me.

I was not strong enough to turn out for the track team that spring, but I gradually regained strength. I could feel the cancer being flushed out of my body. That summer I worked on my dad's construction project. In the fall, I went off to college in Southern California and played on the football team. One day the coach called me in to tell me he couldn't let me play. He had been reading through the player's files and discovered I had had cancer. I was very disappointed. I decided to make a deal with him. I said I would go to the American Cancer Society office in Los Angeles and have a physical. If they would clear me to play, then I would play. He agreed.

I went to the clinic; they examined me and could find no evidence of the cancer and gave me permission to play football. Still, my coach was not convinced. So I went to the City of Hope, a hospital that specializes in cancer treatment. They also examined me and cleared me to play. I had a great season.

The doctor had said that due to the treatments I had undergone, I likely would be sterile. Later, when my wife, Edie, gave birth to Randy, our firstborn, my mother called the doctor who had treated me for Hodgkin's Disease to tell him the good news. The doctor's response was, "Well, maybe he never had cancer." If I didn't have cancer, I was surely very sick with something life-threatening. It was more than a bad case of the flu! If I didn't have cancer, what did I have? Further, the doctor had consulted with a team of doctors concerning my case. Did they all misdiagnose it?

I didn't come to realize the full spiritual significance of the illness until later. After I was healed, I had a fear of recurrence. The doctor told me this fear was called "sophomore's disease." He said that it is the sophomores in medical school who study pathology, and each night they are convinced they have the disease they studied that day! So, with anything unusual I felt physically, I feared the cancer was returning. At such times when this occurred and I was in a bad place spiritually, I would fear facing God and would confess my sin, repent and live righteously. However, when the threat passed, I would revert to my sinful pattern. This was my spiritual lifestyle until I was twenty-eight.

By then I was a seminary graduate, licensed in The Christian and Missionary Alliance and serving as a youth pastor in a C&MA church. I was also married and had a one-year-old son. Spiritually, I had hardened my heart against God and His call to righteousness. I did so because I didn't believe I could, or He could, or anyone could every deliver me from the power of sin. I was a slave to sin. So I lived a hypocritical life, presenting myself as a good Christian on the one hand and living a secret life of concealed sin on the other.

God, in His goodness, dramatically interrupted that pattern. In January of 1970, symptoms appeared, indicating the return of the cancer. A big lump swelled on the side of my neck. Night sweats and fevers were common. My family doctor, knowing my health history, said the Hodgkin's Disease was back. I went through the same repentance pattern as before. When the biopsy report said the mass on my neck was merely a nerve tumor and that I did not have cancer, I went back to my sin.

Then one evening, March 23, 1970, to be exact, I was at home with my wife and son. I was reading a book when I felt a strange sensation in my head. I feared it was a brain hemorrhage. I was certain I was about to die. I reasoned that it was too late to call a doctor or get to the hospital. Nobody could help me. This was different than cancer. This threatened immediate death. Today, if this were to occur, I believe it would be diagnosed as a panic attack. In 1970, that diagnosis was not common. In any case, I was sure I was going to die very soon.

I hadn't prayed in a long time. I thought about whether I believed God existed. I concluded that I did. I wondered what He would do when I died and faced Him, which, I thought, was coming very soon. I remembered back to some Scriptures I had memorized as a child. "If you confess your sins, he is faithful and just to forgive your sins and cleanse you from all unrighteousness" (1 John 1:9). I thought of how unfair it would be for me to be able to be forgiven just before I died, but I didn't want to face the alternative. So, with a little faith, I confessed my sin, until then hidden, and hoped for forgiveness.

By then, my wife knew that something was wrong. I asked her to call an ambulance. I remember thinking that she could pay for it with the death benefit from my life insurance. The ambulance transported me to the hospital. My senior pastor and his wife met us there. The doctor examined me and could find nothing wrong. He asked if I had been experiencing any stress in my life. I replied that there was nothing more than usual. We went back home. I was still convinced that my life was about to end. The pastor and his wife met us back at the house, had prayer with us and left.

At that time, I made a very significant decision. With a great sense of peace flooding in my heart, I decided that I would confess my sin, my hypocritical life, to my wife, Edie. I had just confessed it to God. I was about to die. What did I have to lose by confessing it to my wife? I felt like I owed her honesty.

As I confessed my sinful life to her, she too had a profound spiritual experience. She had been praying that night. Until then, she had feared my death from cancer and didn't want to lose me. By the time 1970 came around and we had been married seven years, she concluded that she could do without me! I had abused her, not physically, but emotionally and spiritually. I was overbearing and argumentative. Being a better arguer than she was, I was able to talk her into and out of things that she knew better than to do or not do. I had manipulated her to the point that she had lost all sense of self-confidence.

So, that crucial night, she prayed, "Lord, take him. I can live without him, and I want to live for You."

When I didn't die as I told her I was going to do, she concluded that God hadn't answered her prayer. But when I confessed to her, she experienced the presence and love of God in a brilliant and dynamic way that completely filled and inspired her. She marks that night as a most important turning point.

We went to bed and fell asleep. I didn't expect to wake up. In fact, I was counting on not waking up. I had confessed my sin to God, reasoning that I could afford to do that because I wouldn't have long to live and for that short span of time I could live a holy life. If I had to face the prospect of living for another day or week or more, I knew I could not live a holy life, and I would be back to despair!

I woke that next morning. I was confused. I just did the rote things. I got up, prepared for and went to the office to work. All the while I was wondering about what I would do when a temptation came along. I knew I would sin again. I had never successfully resisted sin in certain situations, and I knew I would fail again.

Sure enough, midway through the morning I needed to run an errand. Along the route, I faced a temptation. I was very frustrated. I knew it would happen again! And so, with some anger, I said to God, "Here I am. I am facing temptation. Last night You tricked me into confessing my sin with the hope of death. Now I am still alive, and I have to face this! God, I cannot be responsible for this temptation. I cannot bear it! It's Your problem!"

I can't vouch for the theological accuracy of that prayer, but I believe that God heard my heart cry of desperation and delivered me. The next thing I knew, the temptation was gone. It had not turned to sin! For me, this was a first-time experience! I was so profoundly struck by it that I had to pull over to the side of the road and think about it for a while.

As I did, I retraced the events of the recent hours. I concluded that God had broken me, forced me into an impossible situation that caused me to be desperately dependent on Him, at which time I cried out to Him, and He gave me power over the sin. In the next hours and days, I searched the Scriptures for an interpretation of this experience. I realized that God had filled me with His Spirit. He was empowering me to live righteously.

From then on, every time I faced temptation I began to repeat that pattern of desperate prayer and was thereby enabled to overcome. God was giving me lessons on walking in the Spirit. Romans 7, 8, 12 and Galatians 5 were becoming my experience.

Meanwhile, my wife was undergoing her own transformation. We didn't know what was ahead, but we were afraid, excited and ready for whatever came. This experience transformed our marriage, our ministry and our lives.

In retrospect, as I consider this sequence of events in my life, I believe that God had it all arranged in order to glorify Himself in my life. Now I know at least some of what God planned when I came down with cancer in 1959.

Postscript

My son, Randy, is a medical doctor. He received his undergraduate training at Seattle Pacific University, his medical training at Columbia College of Physicians and Surgeons in New York City, which is the oldest medical school in the nation. He completed his residency in General Surgery at Einstein Medical School and Hospital in the Bronx and is now a Fellow in head and neck surgery at Montefiore Hospital in that same borough of New York City.

Due to the fact of his involvement in head and neck surgery, he questioned me about my health history in particular regarding the Hodgkin's Disease and asked if I could procure a copy of my medical records for him to study. After some delay, my oncologist found the records.

Randy asked him what the diagnosis, extent of involvement, prescribed therapy and what the outcome was. They performed a biopsy, and the doctor reported the details and measurements of the swellings. There was a formal diagnosis of Hodgkin's Disease due to the presence of Reid-Sternberg cells. Randy was stunned. The doctor said the prescription for therapy was to apply 1200 rads of radiation therapy to the right side and 900 to the left. He reported that upon receiving that radiation, I went into crisis with metastasis throughout my body. The nodes in my abdomen were so large that they were manually palpable.

Randy asked the oncologist, "Don't you think it is remarkable that my father survived this disease?"

After a pause, he responded, "Yes."

Randy asked further, "If a patient came into your office today and presented these symptoms, even with the current therapies, what chance of survival would you give him?"

After some thought the doctor replied, "Oh, five percent or less."

I have never had medical confirmation of my disease and healing before. All I ever heard was from my mother passing on information she received. I am very encouraged by this development. It defines the work that God did. My healing was indeed a miracle.

CHAPTER

18

Healing—My Personal Journey

By Mitch Schultz

I once preached a sermon on healing. It had the ring of truth and was received with enthusiasm and praise. I felt good about myself after that sermon because I had wonderfully exposited a very difficult issue. I would not be able to preach on healing with such confidence and polished skill if I would be asked to do it now. I do not assert here that I no longer believe that God heals. On the contrary, I believe firmly that God is able to heal. I am simply and honestly confused on why it rarely happens. My belief seems to be clashing with what I observe.

Some weeks ago I was taken to the airport by a student from Toccoa Falls College. We had never met before, so naturally we began to trade information about each other's lives. Everything was going well, and I sensed this would be a productive trip until I shared with her about what Elaine, my wife, had gone through.

"Does your wife speak in tongues?" she asked me.

Suddenly I did not like the direction this was going. Another conversation began, this one a silent one in the conference room of my mind. This woman is obviously going to suggest here that my wife will suddenly be miraculously healed if only she will speak in tongues. I could not believe what I was hearing. Does God play games with us? Does He say, "I will only heal you, if you can somehow manage to place yourself in the category of one of those who speak in tongues?" Is this what God is like?

My first real encounter with the struggle of healing occurred in the first six months of my ministry. Shortly after we arrived in North Carolina, Don, the pastor, took me aside and shared that his wife had been diagnosed with lung cancer. He was saddened but confident that God was going to display His power in the church through her healing. Deep inside, I attempted in vain to drown out the skeptical voice suggesting that it wasn't all that easy. I have seen so many people pump themselves with faith convinced that somehow enough noise, and claims of healing will bring God to move. I was new to the ministry, and so I kept quiet and joined Don in prayer and believed with him that God would do this.

Some weeks later, the elders, deacons and I met with the pastor and his wife to anoint her and pray for her healing. I felt like a bystander, joining these spiritual giants in claiming a healing for God. Would my lack of faith or my skepticism put a damper on the Spirit's power?

The room grew quiet as the attention was now placed upon the fragile figure of the pastor's wife struggling to keep herself propped up in a wheelchair. The silence seemed sacred for a moment as she shared with deep conviction that God had told her she would be healed.

Wow! I thought. *Something is going to happen here.*

She quoted those famous words from Psalm 6:5: "How can I praise you from the grave?

"I am no good in the grave," she concluded. "God wants me well so my life can be a testimony for Him."

The elders and deacons closed in on that dying figure. A prayer was offered in faith, and the oil was dabbed on her forehead. I left that place with a deep certainty that God would heal. He did not. She died several months later.

Today I am confused about healing. What I mean perhaps is, I am more settled with the unanswered questions. I have come to believe that God seems able to accomplish more through someone's suffering than He does through the testimony of healing.

To be honest with you, I have only heard of people being healed. I have never been a first-hand witness to a genuine miracle. When I say a genuine healing, I am referring to an ailment that is completely and visibly reversed with no possible explanation.

Later you will read a good deal about my son's long illness and eventual death with brain cancer. Toward the end of his life, the doctors admitted that nothing more could be done for him. Had he been miraculously healed, it would have shocked the medical world. There has been no recorded recovery from the sort of cancer he suffered.

I believe God sometimes chooses to glorify Himself through the suffering of His servants more than He does through the testimonies of healing. Our western culture denies pain and so God uses it to confront us. We do all we can to run from suffering, so He crosses our paths with it. People like Joni Eareckson Tada have done more to glorify God than a miracle in her life ever could. People identify with pain. Therefore, the strength and the resolve they observe in someone who suffers to remain faithful and true to Christ has a deep and penetrating effect on their lives.

I will never stop praying for healing; neither will I cease to believe in the power of God to heal. My confidence in God is based more on the evidence of Scripture than on the experiences and observations of my life. The testimony of God's power over death and sickness is well documented and anchored in the Scriptures. My confidence in God as able to heal is well grounded, but so is my conviction that He can work just as powerfully when we suffer and are asked to continue suffering. The same God who gives grace to the hurting is the same God who has been proven to heal sickness. In either case, it is God who is at work doing what He wants and what seems best to Him. I can live with that. "For it is God who is at work in you to will and to act according to his good purpose" (Philippians 2:13).

I have come to these conclusions in the midst of deep personal struggle and pain. Only four months after my wife came through a life-threatening operation to remove a brain tumor, our eleven-year-old son was diagnosed as having an inoperable brain tumor. My longing that God would completely heal my wife as she was undergoing intensive speech therapy expanded to embrace the hope that God would also heal our son. He chose not to. What follows is the story of our journey as presented in *Alliance Life* magazine, November 24, 1999 issue.

Not Alone!

Yesterday my family faced the overwhelming realization that our son, Travis, outside of God's intervention, might have only a few months to live. The surgeon who met with us earlier that day was tender but firm in telling us there was nothing further that could be done for him. Travis' tumor had begun to expand further into the brain stem and would, in time, begin to shut down his system.

My wife and I sat on our swinging bench facing the driveway, absorbing all that this meant. Wiping tears from my eyes, I looked up to see a car pulling into the driveway. As it came to a stop, our daughter and youngest son got out and ran toward us. They knew something was not right. My daughter, Breanna, sat on my lap and asked how it had gone that day. "Not well," I told her. "Travis' symptoms will get worse because the tumor is growing again."

Brett, our five-year-old, asked if this meant Travis would die. "Yes," I replied. "Travis will die unless Jesus changes what is happening in his body."

We all wept together on that swinging bench for some minutes, just holding each other. I was touched to see a nine-year-old and a five-year-old so full of emotion and able to cry so easily. *This will help them,* I thought. Then with tears streaming down my face and with a heavy lump in my throat, I looked at each of them and we pledged that we would face this together. "We will be a happy family," I told them. "We will serve Jesus together. God will use this pain to achieve what He wants, and we will be the family He intended us to be." We then prayed together, and the children ran into the house to find Travis.

Come to the Garden

Studying the section in Mark's Gospel that recounts Jesus praying at Gethsemane (Mark 14:32-42) has given me a surge of courage. I find myself standing here longer than I have anywhere on my journey with Christ to the cross. This section records the loneliest and most agonizing moment in the life of our Lord. All sufferers, anyone faced with illness or loss, need to come here to the garden and allow the tears of Jesus to wash the pain away.

The Lord Jesus needed to be at the Garden of Gethsemane to pray. His heart was heavy, and He needed a place to pour out His pain to His Father. He takes His three closest friends with Him so they support Him in His moment of human agony. Mark picks up the mood with such vivid terms . . . "he began to be deeply distressed and troubled" (v. 33). The presence of Peter, James and John allowed Jesus to share the depth of His pain. He tells them, "My soul is overwhelmed with sorrow to the point of death" (v. 34).

The presence of three friends with Jesus was valuable, but we find that it was insufficient. There was something about all this that the disciples could not fully share, and Jesus had to carry it alone. He asked them to stay where they were and "keep watch" or pray with Him and for Him. He goes further ahead as though to suggest that the full agony of the moment was one that He had to experience on His own. The weight of His burden was so heavy, Mark explains, that Jesus fell to the ground (v. 35). There in a posture of helplessness He speaks to His Father. If there were a way out that would still accomplish

God's purpose, then, at that moment, that is what Jesus preferred. "Take this cup from me. Yet not what I will, but what you will" (v. 36).

Some Other Way

Years ago I completely surrendered my life to the Lord Jesus Christ and in doing so gave Him the right to do whatever He wanted with me and through me. At that time, I also dedicated my children to God and accepted that they, too, are His to do with as He wants.

In these last months, I have agonized over Travis' illness and have cried out to God that if there were some other way for Him to accomplish His purposes, then that is what I would prefer. My cry is an echo from the Garden of Gethsemane: *O God, is there not some other way for You to do what You have in mind? Does it have to involve the sickness of my son? O Lord, could You not take this cup from me? I plead with You, Lord, that it would be another way. But, Lord, not my will but Yours is what I ultimately want to subject myself to.*

You see, we endure pain when we accept that a particular trial is necessary for God to achieve what He has in mind. Hebrews 12:2 tells us that Jesus "for the joy set before him endured the cross, scorning its shame" because He accepted that it was the only way for God to carry out His purpose of bringing salvation to mankind.

Only One Source

Jesus returned, perhaps to share with His disciples His newfound courage, and found them sleeping. Disappointed with them, He again left to be with His Father. He pours out His heart again to the One who never sleeps. It is Abba Father who lifts from Jesus the unbearable pain of what He must go through. Christ now has the courage to face the cross.

Finding the disciples sleeping again, Jesus says, "Enough! The hour has come" (Mark 14:41). The word "enough" implies, to some commentators, that the matter was settled or dealt with. Jesus had come to terms with what He must go through and He was ready for it. In that moment of solitary pouring out of pain through prayer, God granted Him the grace to face what was inevitable.

Those of you who have suffered know that there is only one place where that grace to endure can be received. That deep well belongs to our Abba Father, and what He provides can only come in solitary moments when we have poured out our agony before Him.

I am overwhelmed with the support and presence of so many who have "stayed awake" and are "watching" with us. In this trial, I have had many to lean on when the pain seemed unbearable. Yet many have confessed that they cannot fully share the trial to the extent that we as a family have to experience it. There are certain aspects to family pain that can be experienced only by the family. Still, it is God alone who provides the grace reserved especially for the moments of our deepest agony. This grace enables us to go back to those who want to be our pillars of support and declare, "Enough. It is settled." I will go through with this because it is from God and necessary for God to achieve what He has in mind.

“I don’t want to be healed because I want to be with Jesus.” — Travis Schultz

Travis Andrew Schultz died August 22, 1999 in Toccoa, Georgia, of a brainstem tumor. He was twelve.

CHAPTER 19

The Healing of Two Mothers

By Tom Allen

The first mother was known for her outspoken son-in-law. The young man was incessantly putting his foot in his mouth. He had good intentions, but Pete was loud and impetuous. Although he was often the first to commit himself to someone or something, he also had this tendency to bail out when the going got tough.

One day, Pete was alarmed to discover that his mother-in-law had a severely elevated fever. Between 101 and 102. So he did the only thing that made sense. He told Jesus all about it. Immediately, the Savior went to her, took her by the hand and helped her stand up on her feet. In the moment that Christ touched her, the fever completely disappeared.

The second mother was known for her large family. She and her husband had raised ten children. All of them are living for the Lord, and many of them are serving God in full-time ministries. At the age of fifty, Madonna finished her college degree and began teaching first grade. She taught for seventeen years to help her children get through college. But at the age of seventy, this godly woman received some startling news. She had somehow, somewhere, contracted the deadly Hepatitis C virus.

Madonna was given five years to live.

The doctors never discovered the source of this virus. The family was told that Hepatitis C can reside undetected in the human body for decades. Strong medications were applied to no avail. And though many prayers were offered on her behalf, Madonna began to suffer the effects of a degenerative, hardened liver. Almost to the week, the doctors had forecast her death. She died on Mother's Day of 1994 at the age of seventy-five. God did not heal her according to the prayers of friends and family. Or did He?

The first mother was, of course, the mother-in-law of the apostle Peter. The story of her miraculous healing is found in Mark 1:29-34. The second mother was Mrs. Madonna Allen, my mother.

Let's consider these two scenarios with their distinctive outcomes as we look at this matter of divine healing.

The Visit to the Home

"They went with James and John to the home of Simon and Andrew" (Mark 1:29). It's a simple statement about Jesus making a house call. But there's something profound here for all of us. Christ spent a good deal of time meeting with and eating with people in their homes. He was sensitive to the fact that people appreciate and respond to personal attention and concern.

A slick promoter in modern times would try to keep the Savior isolated from common folks—a few photo ops here and there to make it look good, but no real interaction with people. But the Lord Jesus would have rejected his cold, impersonal approach outright. He cared not only for the mingling masses, but also for that single soul.

Christ could have limited His ministry to the mobs that followed Him from town to town. People would have still gathered in great numbers to see and hear Him. His approval ratings would have remained very high. But Jesus took time out for the man in the street and the woman with a dangerously high fever. The King of all kings and Lord of all lords condescended to visit the homes of those He came to redeem.

I can testify today that this same Savior visited my mother at her home on Princeton Court. He was there through it all until her last breath on May 8, 1994. He had promised to be there, and He delivered. How thankful I am to know that Christ cared for her during this painful, emotional ordeal.

Let us not forget the importance of showing personal concern for those who are hurting. In our cold, careless, depersonalized society, it is easy to become apathetic with those who are suffering all around us. People need our love, compassion and hospitality—and we have a need to demonstrate it.

The Victory of the Healing

"Simon's mother-in-law was in bed with a fever, and they told Jesus about her. So He went to her, took her hand and helped her up. The fever left her" (1:30-31b).

According to the verb tense here, Peter's mother-in-law may have been sick for several days. A literal translation would indicate that she was "burning up with the fever." It could have been the flu, pneumonia, an intestinal disease or perhaps even malaria. Given the limited medical assistance that was available at the time, this woman had entered the danger zone.

Her son-in-law had made many blunders in the past, but on this day, he got it right. Simon Peter did something even better that dialing 9-1-1. He told Jesus about his feverish mother-in-law. It reminds me somewhat of a lady who testified that, "I finally gave my husband to the Lord because I couldn't do anything with him!" This is good advice for all of us.

There is tremendous freedom in turning everything and everyone over to Christ. We cannot and do not need to do the saving, the convicting or the healing. These are works of God. We must take our hands off and allow the Lord Jesus to do what only He can do. This is precisely what Peter and the disciples did with this suffering woman.

My family had to offer my mother to the Lord in this way. Though we were frightened with the prospect of Hepatitis C and its devastating, destructive powers, we had to turn her over to Jesus. The doctors were limited in their understanding of this unusual strain. There was no known cure. So like the disciples, we "told Jesus about her."

In the case of Simon's mother-in-law, the result of giving that woman to Christ was dramatic, instant healing: "Jesus took her by the hand and lifted her up and immediately the fever left her." The Savior took the issue of her fever upon Himself, and she was immediately cured. She was returned to her family completely well with a normal body temperature. As we read in Matthew 8:17, "He took up our infirmities and carried our diseases."

God chose a different path for Madonna Allen. When we gave her to Jesus, He decided that He would not give her back to us on this earth. Christ claimed her for His own in paradise. Her death was in itself a wonderful healing because the new body she will receive will not have liver disease. Her new form will be eternal and perfect in every way.

Was it hard to "let go" of this outstanding mother? Indeed it was. But we have the blessed assurance that the best is yet to come for Madonna Allen. As wonderful as she was here on this earth, we haven't yet seen her ultimate state as a child of God. And while she awaits the return of Christ to receive her new body, she is in the conscious presence of the One Who loved her and gave Himself for her.

It is interesting to note that just ten miles from Capernaum was the city of Tiberius. It was known for its famous hot mineral pools which contained curative waters. But these baths were no balm for the bleeding, broken souls who had been carried to Peter's door that evening. Local doctors could not help these diseased and demonized patients. Next to a famous health spa, these desperate people were hopeless and doomed to death if someone did not swiftly intervene.

It's truly a pathetic scene. Dying people with no physician—no help in sight.

Then Jesus came to the door.

When no one else could vindicate or vouch for these suffering souls, Jesus was there. Everyone else had given up. Not Christ. He defended the deaf, the dumb and the demonized. The Savior sided with the sick and the secluded. He still does exactly that.

CHAPTER 20

Learning to Live with the Promise

By Ronald Gifford

It doesn't happen because you decide you're going to have a healing ministry. It happens because people get sick and they ask you to pray for them. Even people whose faith is marginal look for the Lord's help when they're sick.

It started for us here on our second Sunday. Jackie Saunier asked me if the elders would pray for her husband LeRoy, who had just been told he had cancer and that he needed surgery. We gathered before the evening service. There were tears and real concerns. We prayed earnest prayers. The following Tuesday the doctor had cause for pause, and he ordered another biopsy. The next week he suggested that perhaps the first lab tests were flawed because there was absolutely no evidence of cancer now. LeRoy said to him, "Oh yeah! Last week you were ready to take some of my organs! I think there's another reason for the change in the lab results!" This is an Alliance church. There has always been prayer for the sick here.

Four months before that, I was invited by the elders in the Evangelical Free Church in the town where we lived to come and talk to them about anointing the sick. They were between pastors, and they were taking their responsibility as elders very seriously. Their Bible study brought them to James 5. I knew some of them, and I am a graduate of an Evangelical Free seminary, so they were comfortable with me. They also had heard that we anointed with oil, and they wanted to be obedient to the instruction of the Word.

Their questions were simple. What do you do? Do you really put your faith on the line and boldly ask for healing? Do people get healed? How do you handle it when they don't? It was rather exhilarating!

And as I drove home, I found I was profoundly grateful to the Lord that asking for healing had become a common faith stretching exercise and an opportunity for blessing for us. In our first weeks of ministry, the elders met with me for prayer before the evening service, as was our custom. There was a perfect attendance total of three people for our prayer meeting. We were in the Masonic Lodge in Wheaton, Illinois. My wife and children didn't come with me, and when there's only fifty people in the congregation, anybody missing is missed. I explained that Kevin, our little guy, had had rather severe bronchial congestion since about Thursday. He was mostly laying on the floor and panting for breath. The doctor had told us before that he would grow out of that recurring problem by the time he was two, so we weren't worried about it. We set in to praying, and Dave Enlow prayed a wonderful prayer for Kev, asking the Lord to touch him. And I thought, "Isn't that tender! This new friend cares enough for me and my family to pray such a special prayer for my boy."

When I got home from church Kevin was bouncing off the walls! I was surprised, and I asked Joan what was going on. She said, "I don't know what happened. At about ten minutes to six he jumped up off the floor and he's been wired ever since, making up for lost time." We learned something special that day: The Lord has a very tender heart toward His children, and it doesn't have to be a life-threatening event before He wants to touch us with a gift of renewed health. There isn't a great mystery about how this works. When we are sick, we pray.

Praying for Keith Bailey

A couple of years later, the local hospital called, saying that Dr Keith Bailey was asking for me. He had been our District Superintendent, had moved to the national office in Nyack, was back to visit members of his family, but had suffered a serious heart attack. Now he wanted the local pastor to come and pray for him. His book about healing, *The Children's Bread*, had just been released. I had only read the first few pages.

I anointed him and prayed for him. He recovered, and twenty-five years later his heart is still serving him pretty well! But I drove away from that hospital pretty much aware that it can't be the pastor's prayer skills that heal people—the Lord is the Healer, and we are His hands.

Last January I was giving some instruction to our elders about praying for folks at the altar, anticipating a sermon series on the promise of the Holy Spirit as it was articulated in some major Old Testament texts. My lesson was about Jesus giving them authority to heal the sick and cast out demons. I told them he had given that authority to them too when they were commissioned as elders. Robert Eardley was a new elder. He asked the blunt questions. "What if someone comes for prayer like Bob Bunge, who is spiritually my senior, one of the men I look to for mentoring?" I told him to come prepared in his heart to be the instrument of God, and to take the authority that Jesus was giving him, even though he was a young elder in his thirties, and to work with a more seasoned elder until he was comfortable. We also talked about "the laying on of hands," which is listed in Hebrews 6:2 as one of the fundamentals of the faith.

So many people came to the altar the next day that our normal plan to work in pairs had to be scrapped. Robert suddenly was on his own, and he turned to the first one kneeling in his sector. It was Bob Bunge! I expect the Lord was smiling as He watched this new elder gulp and plunge right in. The "pure olive oil from the Holy Land" bottles that I have given each elder is not what heals us, and it is not the skill of the elder—it is Jehovah-Rapha who heals us, the Lord our Healer, so we simply look to Him, and we expect that He hears us when we do.

Praying for Good Gifts

Several years ago when I had a large crop of new elders coming on board, I invited Keith Bailey, who had been our District Superintendent in this District too, to come to an elders and wives retreat and give us some instruction about prayer for the sick. His first hour was about what you would expect—good biblical material and practical help. After the break, Linden and Amy Long started to ask the hard questions. Amy's sister Lisa was a young mom who had had very serious cancer, and nobody was very confident that she would survive.

So how can we pray confidently for healing when God apparently answers only some of the time? We set aside our agenda and spent the rest of the morning wrestling with this one. Dr. Bailey began to talk about God's bigger purpose for us, which includes special blessing in times of suffering and eternity in heaven. I think we learned that morning the importance of seeking to sense from the Lord what He intended to do in each case, like Elisha expecting that the Lord would reveal to him what was going on with the distraught woman (2 Kings 4:27). We also decided that we would stay in contact with those who come for prayer, praying for them again if there wasn't an apparent improvement, perhaps asking three times like the apostle did, seeking to sense together what blessing the Lord has for each one.

One Sunday a young woman named Wendy Larson was at the altar at the conclusion of our second service. Several were gathered around as she told about her impending surgery that week to correct her jaw's under-bite—that's breaking the jaw and resetting it. We usually ask the seeker to pray first, then others offer their prayers. One of the reasons we like to pray in pairs or groups is so that while others are praying, the one with the oil especially can earnestly seek to discern what the Lord wants to do here. I had the oil that morning, and I had no sense of guidance from the Lord. So I prayed a prayer that put our sister in His good hands, encouraging her to yield her life to Him as we prayed, for whatever good gift He had for her.

When everyone disbursed, my young colleague, Pete Hise, stayed to talk about it. He said to me, "I don't think that's right. I think the Lord wanted to touch her and heal her." It was a very strong impression—the word of knowledge that often sets up "the prayer of faith" that James said is key. I asked him why he didn't interrupt me, or add his prayers to mine. He said that he had joined the prayer circle late, and he wasn't sure if someone else had already prayed a strong prayer for healing. Wendy went back to the doctor the next day. He showed her Friday x-rays and Monday x-rays, and he said, "I don't know what happened to you over the weekend, but you have a Class A jaw here. You certainly don't need surgery!" Of course the whole church celebrated that one for a while! And we learned the importance of tuning our ears to the voice of God, to seek to sense what he wants to do.

Women Pray Too

Lexington is a medical community. There are lots of medical practitioners in our church. We have never had any tension between divine healing and the practice of medicine, accepting modern medicine as one of God's good gifts. One doctor told me once, "God is the only One who can make people better. That amazing recovery that happens in a person's body is a gift of God. We work with it as best we know how."

Some of our hospitals here are provided by Christian people who know how to extend gifts of mercy in the name of Christ. Once when I went to Central Baptist Hospital to see Bill Suvanto, whose heart problems were serious again, I walked into his room just as the doctor was raising the paddles to give him the electric shock that might stabilize his pulse rate. I felt very awkward, it seemed like an inappropriate time to pop in. There were half a dozen people in medical greens standing around the bed ready to assist.

I wore a clergy tag. The doctor looked at me and asked, "Are you this man's pastor?" I admitted that I was. Then he said, "Stand back everybody, and let this man do his work first." I prayed a strong prayer, for him and for them. Then they continued. Bill came home a couple of days later. We were learning that the beautiful people God gives to care for the sick are part of the answer to our prayers too.

So our circle of people with healing gifts is wider than the elders. One Sunday morning a young woman named Amy Baczkowski asked for anointing and prayer. We gathered in the prayer room—about twelve elders and her husband standing around the chair where Amy sat, and we asked her about her physical need. It was an infertility story, rather awkward for a woman to tell a circle of such august men! We prayed for her. A month later she was pregnant, and her son Gabriel is God's special gift. But when she walked out the door, we looked at each other and said, "We will never do that again." When we pray for women, we are sure that there are women in the prayer circle. We have learned that some of our women know how to pray for healing!

Lessons in Life

I spent some vacation time a few years ago with a good friend who is a physician in family practice. I asked him what had changed in medicine in the twenty-five years that he had been a doctor. He said the instance of allergies has dramatically increased. And he said that psychosomatic illnesses are now more than half of what he sees. When I asked for explanation, he simply said that most of our diseases now are the results of stress, or that recovery from real physical problems needs a lifestyle adjustment as part of the healing prescription. That insight has been reinforced in our experience here:

In the last week of January, 1997, I came down with the flu. Well, it seemed like the flu on Monday. On Thursday I wondered why it wasn't going away. By the first week in March I was in my doctor's office, and we began a pretty extensive round of tests. I tried to pretend that I could carry on, but it was getting hard. Joan and I took a group to Israel, and I just didn't have the stamina to keep up. In September I really crashed hard. More tests that followed symptomatic clues revealed nothing. Dave Winkle, my doctor, studied my case intensely. Then one day in his office he told me it must be Chronic Fatigue Syndrome, which is diagnosed by eliminating a lot of other things and matching a profile of common symptoms. It's a virus that damages brain and CNS functions. One's immune system is damaged too so that lots of other things go haywire. The patient is left with making lifestyle adjustments, making the best of a bad deal.

My church was very generous to us. I continued to preach, though there were times when I couldn't do much more. I had to avoid the more stressful things that came up at church, and we had a lot of them. I was suffering more than I told anyone, and in time the church suffered too.

Then time came to preach about healing. I do that every other year in the weeks after Easter and anticipating Pentecost. Now I'm preaching while sitting on a stool. Everybody in the place knows that I'm sick. And I asked them to turn in their Bibles to James 5. We spent five weeks there, looking at it line upon line. I sent them home after the first week, urging a week's preparation before anybody came for anointing, giving them some guidelines to help them come ready.

After preaching the second sermon, I opened the altar and told them that I would be the first to kneel before the Lord seeking His healing touch. There were a lot of folks gathered around me, and I was aware of their love and concern for me. But I wasn't listening to what they were saying, because I was intently talking to the Lord. I told Him, "I have really learned a lot in these sixteen months. These 'going deeper' lessons have been very precious. But Lord I'm so tired, and my wife has lived with such a strain, and it is clear that my church is affected by my weak leadership. Can we be done with this now?" And He said to me, "OK, I'm going to give you a healing touch today, *but don't go back to being stupid like you were before*." It was pretty clear to me that that was a rebuke! I knew before I got up off my knees that He had touched me though, because I could think clearly again, and my arms and legs no longer ached. My rather public illness had become an occasion for the whole church to learn to expect both healing and deeper level help.

The word of the Lord in that rebuke is important. As we have wrestled in prayer for people who are sick, we are increasingly aware of how much of our lifestyle indulgences affect our health. Part of our healing often includes making adjustments in diet and exercise. Sometimes it's faith adjustments—

frankly, worrying makes us sick. And (for me and many others) lots of us need to make adjustments in our balance between work and rest. We also learned that month that we can't ignore the "confess your sins to each other" line in the instructions. When we go to someone's home to pray for them, we take more time to talk about all of these things than we did before. When we pray for them at the altar or in the Prayer Room after a service, we commonly ask for a brief description of the need that brings them for prayer, and then we ask, "Is there anything that you need to confess today, anything that needs to be taken care of, so that the Lord will be free to give you His blessing?" It still feels a little invasive, but we have told our people to expect it, and to accept that confession isn't always a private matter. Often what the Lord has for us is not just healing—His blessing will include an adjusted life.

Our latest lesson in how all of this works is the Lord's reminder that He loves His children and He simply wants to give us good things. Here is the story:

Joan and I were leading a leadership development small group. I was out of town one week, and Joan or one of the others could have led the next lesson. She decided instead that the group was overdue for a "sharing and prayer" night. Her instinct was right. The deep personal needs poured out. Among those great young people were couples living with the private grief of infertility. They wept as they told how it hurt. I'm glad Joan was there to lead it. We had three babies in three years, so we have not felt that deep hurt. But because she is a woman, she could weep with them so much better than I could. She could give them her faith too, because over the years we have often had our prayers for the gift of children answered.

They poured their hearts out to the Lord and prayed for one another. By that summer they were announcing to the church family that one couple found their application for another baby from China had been put on a fast track and that a remarkable change in stock options value was going to pay for it; three other couples were pregnant, one after ten years of waiting; one of the others was Dan & Amy Baczkowski, a second answer to prayer for them; the third couple who already had three children and were merely praying for the others! The blessings just spill over!

We have more to learn. We need to find a way to make these seeking prayers more public more often, so the whole church family can be part of it. We also need to encourage the faith level of the entire congregation—not just the folks with physical needs. We're concerned to read that once Jesus "could not do any miracles there . . . amazed at their lack of faith" (Mark 6:5-6). Our worship is stronger than ever, and that helps. When we earnestly recognize and honor our Lord, He comes to us, and "the power of the Lord was present for him to heal the sick" (Luke 5:17).

We need to step up to the challenge in the second part of that authority that he gives and take on the demonic more assertively too.

Ezekiel preached his "Heart of Stone—Heart of Flesh" message promising the Spirit on two occasions. In chapter 11, he told them that they needed what only God could give. In chapter 36, he was telling them that the other reason he wanted to do all this is so that his name would be honored out there.

Jesus sent His disciples out with gifts of healing to accompany their announcement that His kingdom had arrived. Perhaps it's time that we step up to this challenge too and make prayer for the sick part of our outreach—one of the good gifts of the kingdom that we can share. There aren't many sick people who would turn down a prayer. Perhaps this apostolic outreach theme ought to be brought right up into our stressed-out generation as an introduction to a new and better life that is rich and full and only the beginning of what will go on into eternity.

Divine Healing:
Looking to the Future

CHAPTER

21

Preparing to Receive Divine Healing

By Richard Sipley

So he cried out to the LORD, and the LORD showed him a tree. When he cast it into the waters, the waters were made sweet.

There He made a statute and an ordinance for them, and there He tested them, and said, "If you diligently heed the voice of the LORD your God and do what is right in His sight, give ear to His commandments and keep all His statutes, I will put none of the diseases on you which I have brought on the Egyptians. For I am the LORD who heals you." (Exodus 15:25-26, NKJV)

Is any among you sick? Let him call for the elders of the church, and let them pray over him, anointing him with oil in the name of the Lord. And the prayer of faith will save the sick, and the Lord will raise him up. And if he has committed sins, he will be forgiven. Confess your trespasses to one another, and pray for one another, that you may be healed. The effective, fervent prayer of a righteous man avails much. (James 5:14-16, NKJV)

God established the first ordinance of healing for His people before the first church was erected in the wilderness. In James 5, God established it again for the New Testament church, so that the Lord's healing power might always be available to all the members of His body through the end of the age. The various parts of this ordinance are simple but very important. These parts constitute instructions for both the elders and the ones who are sick. If we intend to participate in this ordinance, we do well to give careful heed to these instructions.

The Sickness

The first thing we notice in this passage is "the sickness" of the person seeking healing. There are at least four basic kinds of sickness that Jesus dealt with in the Bible account. In Matthew 4:23 and 24 we read

> And Jesus went about all Galilee, teaching in their synagogues, preaching the gospel of the kingdom, and healing all kinds of sickness . . . among the people. . . . His fame went throughout all Syria; and they brought to Him all sick people who were afflicted with various diseases and torments, and those who were demon-possessed, epileptics, and paralytics; and He healed them. (NKJV)

Here you see infectious diseases, demon possession, mental illness and nervous disorders. Jesus healed all kinds of sickness. There is no limitation to Him. He is just the same today.

Behind these four kinds of illness there are many causes. It is important that we consider some of them briefly, as our healing often hinges on carefully dealing with the cause.

1. *Infections.* Where there is infection, there is some harmful form of life invading the body. This should be defeated or destroyed by rebuke in Jesus' name, as Jesus did with a fever which afflicted Peter's mother-in-law.

2. *Birth Defects.* Jesus healed these for God's glory as He did with the man born blind. These healings usually require creative action from God and are miraculous.

3. *Accidents.* Many of these kinds of illnesses are brought on by carelessness. In that case, repentance and common sense is in order.

4. *Abuse of the Body.* In our day, this is a very common cause of sickness. Many times we are sick because we have knowingly abused the body which God has given to us. Some abuse their bodies by overeating or eating too much rich food. Others do it with tobacco, or too much coffee, or constant use of various prescription drugs. Some neglect proper sleep and exercise. Others develop ulcers, colitis or heart trouble from ungodly emotions. If our sickness is caused by sinful abuse, we must repent or it is useless to come for anointing and prayer. God is not mocked.

5. *Divine Discipline.* The Bible is clear in both the Old and New Testaments that some sickness is a direct discipline of God. There are many cases. I will list two for your consideration: Numbers 12:1-16 and First Corinthians 11:27-32. If we ask, "How may I know if my sickness is disciplinary?" I answer, "Ask God about it."

If He is disciplining us, He will be quick to let us know and will even tell us why. At that point we should confess our sin, repent and begin to obey. That will be the first step toward healing. If someone should say that a loving God would not chasten us, I again reply that a loving God is the very One who will chasten us, for He says in Hebrews 12:6, "Whom the LORD loves He chastens, And scourges every son whom He receives." The Lord wounds in love, and He binds up in love. Let us trust in Him.

6. *Satan or Demons.* Satan and evil spirits cause both physical and mental illness. Satan made Job sick from his head to his feet. Satan had bound a humpbacked woman, as recorded in Luke 13 for eighteen years. Jesus loosed her. The maniac of Gadara in Mark 5 and the epileptic boy of Mark 9 were both cases of mental illness caused by demon power. Jesus delivered them both, by first dealing with the evil spirits. It is important to recognize this cause for if it exists, there will probably not be healing until it is dealt with in the name and authority of Jesus Christ.

7. *Mental Problems.* I am deeply convinced that all real mental illness is caused by either a definite physical problem of some kind or by satanic or demonic activity. All other so-called mental illness is really spiritual in origin and must be dealt with as such, or there will not be healing. Guilt, sinful anger and ungodly fear are behind much that passes for mental illness. These are spiritual problems and must be dealt with by confession, repentance, faith and obedience.

8. *Old Age.* The only way to avoid old age is to die young. Nevertheless, there is help in Jesus for the aged, as they practice common sense and develop a

sweet and joyful disposition through the Spirit-filled life.

I have gone to some length mentioning these causes because it is important to deal with these matters in the presence of God before the anointing and prayer. Many are prayed for that are not healed. Why? Has God changed? Certainly not! I believe the main reason for failure is the lack of careful, honest, scriptural preparation.

The Call

"Is anyone among you sick? Let him call for the elders of the church" (James 5:14, NKJV). This settles the matter of responsibility. You are responsible to ask for anointing and prayer when you are sick. "Let him call for the elders of the church, and let them pray . . ." (5:14, NKJV). Why did God put it that way? Oh, someone says, "I thought if you were sick, that the pastor was just supposed to come to your home and anoint you and pray for God to heal you." No. You are to take the initiative. Why? Because divine healing is not religious magic. It is a real exchange between an honest believing heart and the fact of a loving God. To lay hands suddenly on any man and pray for his healing with little or no preparation very often makes a mockery of both prayer and healing and does more harm than good. The Christian who is sick is responsible to prepare his heart and life carefully for God's touch, and then to ask for the anointing and prayer, fully expecting that the Lord will raise him up.

The Elders

Next we see that the elders are to lay hands on

the sick and to anoint with oil in the name of the Lord. What is this laying on of hands? It is, I believe, the using of a Spirit-filled elder as a minister of the truths and power of God. He is not there as an inanimate object would be. He is a gifted servant of Christ, placed there at that time to counsel, guide, correct, reprove, bind evil spirits and pray the prayer of faith for the sick person. We must not take this ministry lightly, either in the doing of it or in coming to receive it. What of the oil? It is a type of the Holy Spirit who brings the life of Jesus right into our bodies to meet our every need.

The Prayer of Faith

Then comes the prayer of faith. What is the prayer of faith? It is a prayer based on two things. First, it must be based on the Word of God. The Word of God is its foundation. Romans 10:17 tells us that faith comes by the Word of God. Before we come for anointing and prayer, we ought to search the Scriptures and be convinced in our own minds that the Bible teaches divine healing for this day.

The second base for the prayer of faith is the witness of the Holy Spirit. The letter kills, but the Spirit gives life. Knowing what the Bible teaches is not enough. Our Bible belief must be quickened into living faith by the witness of the Holy Spirit. The fruit of the Spirit is faith (Galatians 5:22). We cannot force the witness of the Spirit; therefore, we cannot force faith. We cannot make ourselves believe. Healing comes from God. It is divine healing. God will not hand this power to us to use as we see fit. This does not mean that God is a respecter of persons. It only means that God knows all there is to know about each individual case, and God will turn our Bible belief into living faith when and if He sees that it is proper to do so.

Let us study God's Word and then wait before Him with a trusting obedient attitude until the witness of God's Spirit is clear in our hearts. Then let us come and be healed. This should encourage those who have been prayed for but have not been healed to go back to their Bibles and back to their knees to seek God's face for His direction and will in the matter. Then, under His leading, they may come for prayer again and be healed.

Confess Your Sins

Another important step in preparation for this healing ordinance is the matter of dealing with sin. "If he has committed sins, he will be forgiven. Confess your tresspasses to one another, and pray for one another, that you may be healed" (James 5:15-16, NKJV). It is very important that your heart be completely right with God when you come for healing. Won't God ever heal anyone if there's any sin in their life? I am not prepared to say that. I have seen some remarkable things. I would not presume to limit God. I would not say what God will not do. I will say that if you want to be sure you are on solid ground, you better come in the way God has set forth in His Word. God says to confess your sins. If our heart condemns us not, then we have confidence before God. It is unlikely you can exercise living faith toward God for your healing if you knowingly retain unconfessed sin in your life. Let us then confess every sin to God and also to man where it is indicated by the particular offense. The witness of the Spirit will not come to a rebellious heart, and the witness of the Spirit is necessary for healing.

Divine Healing!

Finally, it is to be in the name of the Lord. It is to be in Jesus' name. Let me emphasize again that the healing we're talking about is divine healing. It is not faith healing. There are many cults which do in fact produce some kinds of healings through the power of the natural human mind. This is not the power of God. Divine healing is from God alone. Of course, it is by faith in Him. Peter said, "It is by faith in His name that this man stands here whole before you all" (Acts 4:10, NKJV). But Peter also said that it was the God of our fathers who healed him. Our text states that "the Lord will raise him up" (James 5:15, NKJV). Not the pastor, but the Lord. Not the elders, but the Lord. Not the evangelist, but the Lord. He is our Healer. We must look to the Lord Himself. Let us ask God to look upon us. Let us bow before that gaze with honest obedient hearts until we have the witness. Then let us fix our eyes upon Jesus Christ alone and look to Him until He meets our every need.

These are some simple instructions to assist us in preparing for the ordinance of healing. It we are serious about our healing, we shall certainly take time for this careful preparation. Then let us come for anointing and prayer, expecting to be healed.

Personal Inventory

What is my physical problem? Please be exact and detailed.

What do I want God to do for me physically? Again, be exact and detailed.

What are my reasons for wanting to be healed? Please list them in order of importance in your own thinking.

Please meditate prayerfully on the following Scriptures: First Corinthians 6:12-20; Romans 12:1-2; First Corinthians 7:3-4; Second Corinthians 6:14-7:1. Now list the changes God wants you to make in the use of your body.

Please meditate prayerfully on the following Scriptures: Romans 12:9-10, 14-21; Matthew 5:21-24; Matthew 18:15-35. Now list the names of those persons with whom God wants you to make adjustments, and next to the name, what God wants you to do.

Name what God wants you to do.

Write below a solemn covenant with God in which you give Him your body unreservedly to be used for His glory whether by life or by death!

Please sign your name here:

Please deliver this inventory to the elders for their study and prayer at least one week before the time of your anointing and prayer.

CHAPTER 22

A.B. Simpson and the "Friday Meetings"

By K. Neill Foster

The "Friday Meetings" on divine healing which were carried on for many years in the Gospel Tabernacle in New York City flowed out of the pastoral heart of Albert Benjamin Simpson. Those events which transpired in the very first church of The Christian and Missionary Alliance continue to have significance and meaning today.

The dramatic personal healing of A.B. Simpson is well-known. From the peril of a life-threatening heart condition, God was pleased to intervene in his life, healing him and giving him the strength to climb a mountain the very next day.

From that time forward, Presbyterian A.B. Simpson became a believer in and practitioner of divine healing. Typically, he made a written covenant with God that he would advance the gospel of healing as a part of his ministry from that time forward. He was true to his word, and he did it mainly through his Friday Meetings.

That covenant, duly signed, would cost him dearly in the years to come. Some mocked, others ridiculed.

But the covenant to the ministry of healing would open the doors of deliverance to many thousands. Indeed, the healings recorded in this book are, in part, the fruit of Simpson's healing ministry.

Old Orchard Convention

Similarly, the Old Orchard Convention is part of Alliance history. The missionary and deeper life conventions at the camp ground were an annual impetus to the worldwide vision of its leader.

My wife and I have visited Old Orchard, Maine. The camp ground is now owned by the Salvation Army. There, among the stately trees in a natural ampitheater, untouched still today, the gospel of healing was preached. There in the open air, dramatic healings took place—even the opening of blind eyes.

The healing ministry at Old Orchard was also duplicated in the missionary conventions promoted by The Christian and Missionary Alliance all over America. For years in our history, conventions were presented in the major cities of America and Canada. Always there was a faithful presentation of divine healing as part of the Fourfold Gospel.

The Gospel Tabernacle

In the Gospel Tabernacle in New York, the ministry of healing gained prominence in what were termed the "Friday Meetings." These Friday events focused on the ministry of healing and prayer for the sick. They were a regular feature of Simpson's pastorate in New York.

There are still remnants of that ministry today in Manhattan. Today one may visit the old Gospel Tabernacle sanctuary at 266 West 44th Street, now

John's Pizzeria. The pizza is good, though all of the beer served there would certainly offend the first pastor of that sanctuary. One can still see the stained glass, the etched symbols of the Fourfold Gospel, the iron chandeliers still decorated with the cross and the plaques on the walls which remind patrons that it was once a house of prayer.

A huge and modern mural now adorns the wall back of where Simpson once had his pulpit. Gone is the memorable statement on the same wall: "The LORD thy God in the midst of thee is mighty" (Zephaniah 3:17, KJV). What a great theme it was. No wonder the Friday Meetings flourished. No wonder a worldwide missionary movement flowed out of that sanctuary.

Yesterday, Today and Forever

The days of A.B. Simpson are gone. But God is not. "Jesus Christ is the same yesterday and today and forever" (Hebrews 13:8). In some ways, at least, the testimonials in this volume all spring from the Gospel Tabernacle and the anointed ministry of A.B. Simpson.

Today, the ministry of healing is not as vigorous as it once was. Some of these testimonials are written by those who have finished their earthly journey. Others are very contemporary. And there are efforts to renew this marvelous ministry.

I am part of one of those efforts. During pastoral transition in 1999, as the elders at Immanuel Alliance Church in Mechanicsburg, Pennsylvania, we instituted our very own "Friday Meetings," only they were on Sunday nights once a month. When our new pastor, Rev. Terry Smith, arrived on the scene, he wanted to continue them. Interest and attendance are encouraging, and our band of intercessors is growing. Some healings have taken place. We are expecting more.

Since this book, *Healing Voices,* was conceptualized, my passion as one of the editors has been that through it a new witness would be raised up to affirm that a regular and determined ministry of healing is very much a part of what the Alliance has been for many years and can still be today.

The power of the Lord is still present to heal. It is time to shout once more in thousands of our churches, "The LORD thy God in the midst of thee is mighty."

The believing heart will find it so.

Participating Authors

Note: All of the authors are related to The Christian and Missionary Alliance (C&MA).

Rev. Tom Allen is an evangelist of the C&MA.

Alliance Life contributors are Dorothy F. Barefoot, Adienne Klassen, Nelson Price, Marsha McQueen and Laurel West.

Dr. Keith Bailey is a minister-at-large in the C&MA.

Dr. James Davey is the senior pastor of Village Church, Shell Point, Fort Myers, Florida.

Dr. V. Raymond Edman was President and Chancellor of Wheaton College, Wheaton, Illinois.

Dr. K. Neill Foster is President/Publisher at Christian Publications, Inc., Camp Hill, Pennsylvania.

Dr. Ronald Gifford is the senior pastor of Elberta Alliance Church, Elberta, Alabama.

Rev. Sanford Hashimoto is a missionary with the C&MA in Brazil.

Rev. Jesse Jespersen is pastor of L'Alliance, Cretienne e Missionnaire, Lévis, Québec.

Dr. Peter Nanfelt is the President of the C&MA.

Dr. Timothy Owen is the senior pastor of The Alliance Church, Ellensburg, Washington.

Rev. H.P. Rankin was a pastor and evangelist of the C&MA.

Rev. Mitch Schultz is a missionary with the C&MA in Great Britain.

Rev. Clarence Shrier was an evangelist of the C&MA.

Dr. A.B. Simpson was the founder of the C&MA.

Rev. Richard Sipley is formerly the senior pastor of Hillsdale Alliance Church, Regina, Saskatchewan.

Dr. A.C. Snead was Foreign Secretary of the C&MA.

Rev. W.G. Weston was an evangelist of the C&MA.

Bibliography

Bailey, Dr. Keith M. *Divine Healing: The Children's Bread.* Camp Hill, PA: Christian Publications, Inc., 1977, pp. 157-163.

Fant, Rev. David J., editor. *Modern Miracles of Healing*. Harrisburg, PA: Christian Publications, Inc., 1943. (The articles by Edman, pp. 23-28; Rankin, pp. 84-89; Snead, pp. 45-50; and Weston, pp. 33-38; appear in this book.)

Shrier, Clarence. *My God Can Do Anything!* Beaverlodge, Alberta, Canada: Horizon House Publishers, 1975, pp. 53-61.